QUALITY OF WORK LIFE ASSESSMENT

QUALITY OF WORK LIFE ASSESSMENT

A Survey-Based Approach

JAMES L. BOWDITCH
Boston College

ANTHONY F. BUONO
Bentley College

 Auburn House Publishing Company
Boston, Massachusetts

Library of Congress Cataloging in Publication Data

Bowditch, James L.
   Quality of work life assessment.

   Includes bibliographical references and index.
   1. Employee attitude surveys.   2. Psychology, Industrial.
I. Buono, Anthony F.   II. Title.
HF5549.5.A83B68   658.3′142   82-3945
ISBN 0-86569-067-7   AACR2

Printed in the United States of America

In memory of Edgar F. Huse, 1924–1981
In honor of Mary Lou Huse

PREFACE

Initially we set out to chronicle the events that routinely take place in employee surveys. Although several related books were available, we found few sources that provided both sufficient detail about the survey process as well as bibliographic information about specific phases of survey-based organization development. As we continued our research, it became more apparent that this particular approach in organization development was not adequately represented by existing models, and that it might be helpful to present the conceptual scheme employed in our research as a guide for human resources managers and organizational consultants.

Basically, our book is a reference guide to survey-based organization development. Although we outline a particular model, it is clear that each time a survey is undertaken, there may be variations on this theme, depending on the needs of the organization. We wished to show the flexibility in this process, but at the same time provide guidance useful to both surveyors and interpreters of survey data.

The main difference between this volume and the many related books is that it combines the elements of a practitioner's manual, a research guide, and an academic sourcebook. Different readers will, therefore, find different sections most appropriate to their particular interests. Those wishing to use the book in conjunction with a survey-based organization development course will want to read the first two chapters carefully before proceeding. The first chapter sets the rationale of survey-based organization development. It is heavily referenced and outlines the reasons why many organizations are concerned about the motivations, feelings, and attitudes of their employees. The second chapter discusses survey feedback as a viable approach for organizations to detail employee perceptions of the quality of their work life. It lists the uses of survey feedback in organizational life and develops a descriptive model of this process.

The practitioner may wish to skim over the first two chapters, but use the rest of the book as a guide to planning the activities that are necessary prior to, during, and after a survey. Chapters 3, 4, and 5 describe in detail the sequence of events for comprehensive survey-based organization development. While it often appears that certain steps may be omitted to reduce the amount of effort it takes to develop and administer a survey, we have found that organizations need time to anticipate a survey, and practitioners need time to create instruments which truly tap the issues germane to the particular organization.

The last chapter is an outline of the potentialities and limitations of survey feedback in dealing with quality of work life issues. Most organization development efforts depend on having valid data about the particular organization. Attitudes made known through survey research are an excellent basis for further interventions. This chapter discusses briefly some of the more common interventions and their limitations.

Finally, an appendix on statistical techniques useful in the analysis of survey data is included. If an organization is sufficiently large that a sample survey is preferable to a population survey, practitioners must know whether the differences obtained in the subsamples are significant or chance events. The appendix provides descriptions of types of higher order statistical analyses that might be performed on sample data.

Our hope is that the book will be useful to students of and practitioners in today's complex organizations.

J.L.B.
A.F.B.

ACKNOWLEDGMENTS

When a book is written, there are always a number of people to thank for their help in making the project a success. Our situation is no different from most authors; we are particularly grateful for the support we have been given through our institutions, Bentley College and Boston College. Our colleagues, especially the late Edgar Huse, John W. Lewis III, Dalmar Fisher, Jean Bartunek, R.S.C.J., Judith Gordon, Alan Thayer, Davis Dyer, Frank Dooher, Eleanor Moushegian, Maureen Ball, Joseph O'Connor, Aaron Nurick, Judith Kamm, Arthur Walker, Baba Verma, Ed Marshall, the late Glen Gish, and Litsa Nicolaou-Smokovitis have directly or indirectly contributed to the final product.

We are indebted to Pearl Alberts, the Reference Librarian, and to Rhoda Channing, the School of Management librarian at Boston College for helping us find the references we needed. We wish to acknowledge Peter Kelly, Barbara Haroz, and Douglas Lifton, our graduate assistants who spent time making computer runs or xerox runs in our behalf. Many thanks are due to Paulette Kidder, Kumiko DiSalvo, and Grace O'Donnell, our secretaries, and to Jeanne Levesque, our work study assistant, who turned out near flawless manuscript starting with very flawed copy. We also thank John J. Neuhauser, Jeremiah O'Connell, and John Burns, our deans, who did not throw away the keys to our copying machines, despite more than adequate provocation.

We are grateful for the support of our academic vice presidents, the Rev. J. Allan Panuska, S.J., and Dr. Jack Nichols, and our respective presidents, the Rev. J. Donald Monan, S.J., and Dr. Gregory Adamian. Their encouragement for this sort of undertaking was very supportive.

Finally, our wives, Felicity and Mary Alice, provided much encouragement, forgiveness, and occasional moans and groans which kept us at this task.

J.L.B.
A.F.B.

ix

CONTENTS

LIST OF FIGURES

LIST OF TABLES

Chapter 1

INTRODUCTION

During the 1970s work-related attitudes demanded increasing managerial attention. In the view of many current social observers, job satisfaction has declined to the extent that "blue-collar blues" and "white-collar woes" have become commonplace terms—indicating that worker attitudes will continue to be an important concern during the 1980s as well. Indeed, discussion on this issue has ranged from such popular books as Studs Terkel's *Working* to the government's task force report *Work in America*. The perspectives put forth in these sources strongly suggest that societal change is occurring at a much faster rate than organizational change. Consequently, dissatisfaction and even alienation from the work place are accelerating.

Other critics argue that these discussions of impersonalized and dehumanized work are more representative of academic reflection than of what is actually taking place in the business world.[1] In fact, these individuals argue that worker satisfaction remained highly positive during the last decade. Thus the issue of worker satisfaction remains somewhat controversial, and the debate continues to stimulate a high level of concern at both the organizational and societal levels.

From an organizational perspective, the traditional assumption underlying many of these concerns is that a dissatisfied worker is a less productive one. The association between satisfaction and performance that dominated much of the theoretical and pragmatic interest in industrial psychology through the early 1960s, however, has recently been questioned because of its dependence on inconclusive research findings. Some studies have found that job satisfaction results in higher levels of productivity in the work place; other

1

empirical efforts, by contrast, have produced contradictory results. This research has subsequently influenced a more critical view of the importance of worker satisfaction and other job-related attitudes.

The Importance of Worker Attitudes in Contemporary Society

Today managerial and scholarly focus is shifting back toward worker attitudes. According to a common, though still controversial, viewpoint, negative attitudes are among the "culprits" underlying our productivity problems. Many social observers look at worker attitudes in American society and raise the Japanese model as an example of how positive attitudes can lead to a more effective work force.[2] The prevailing thought is *still* that high satisfaction leads to high productivity, in spite of the inconclusive research. Participative management tools such as Japan's "quality circle," Volvo's sociotechnical systems approach (in use at its automotive plant in Kalmar, Sweden), and General Motors' use of semi-autonomous work groups in its Tarrytown, New York, plant as well as some of its southern plants further point out the perceived potential that employee involvement in the work process can have on organizational output. Although differences in cultural settings and orientations obviously limit the extent to which any of these models can be directly transferred from one society to another, the significance of the participative worker-organizational relationship is almost universally accepted. As such, the measurement, understanding, and monitoring of employee attitudes toward the work place and job-related functions have re-emerged as important managerial activities.

On a societal level, worker dissatisfaction has a number of implications for quality of life issues. Public expectations have evolved to the point where business is beginning to be evaluated on social and ethical grounds as well as on the traditional economic and legalistic performance criteria.[3] Indeed, many individuals feel that organizations have a primary responsibility to their employees, especially considering the substantial portion of one's lifetime that is spent in the work role.[4] Efforts to reduce job-related stress, ways to cope with worker burnout, and programs to assist employees in their career development all reflect the convergence of work and quality of life issues.

Recommendations for such large-scale organizational programs of change, however, cannot be based merely on speculative opinions, anecdotal references, media reports, or single-case examples.[5] In fact, the present tendency in many organizations to employ the latest management fad or "tool" usually results in hastily conceived, unproductive programs and unnecessary resource use. By contrast, the systematic collection of relevant information can provide the basis for a thorough analysis of organizational processes and structures in today's society. Indeed, if collected in an insightful and careful manner, the data which are generated can provide a useful perspective on the nature of life in an organization.

One of the methods of analysis often utilized is referred to as *survey feedback* or *survey-guided development*, a process by which data are collected, analyzed, and fed back to the participants for discussion and further evaluation. Unfortunately, although the use and development of a survey methodology have characterized a growing portion of empirical efforts in the social sciences, this trend has only begun to be reflected in organizational use. In fact, the design, implementation, and interpretation of such surveys in an organizational context are often characterized by disjointed efforts rather than any coordinated, integrated research plan. Of course, such haphazard surveys have generally resulted from a lack of informative guidelines focused toward managers rather than any sort of organizational neglect. However, many of the resulting attempts at this type of data collection have consequently been less than satisfactory. This book attempts to fill part of this methodological void.

Since this book is oriented toward the practitioner in contemporary organizations, the discussion and format are more pragmatic than theoretical in nature. The remainder of Chapter 1 delves into such issues as organizations as open systems, the worker-organization relationship, and employee motivation, but the focus is primarily on the implications and consequences of these phenomena rather than on theoretical developments or model building. Moreover, these management science perspectives will be presented and analyzed in terms of the basis and importance of studying work-related attitudes and opinions.

Organizations as Open Systems

Organizations in contemporary society are complex entities. They consist of a number of elements, each with its own attributes, which interact to varying degrees and with varying outcomes. Moreover, this interaction occurs within a larger environmental context. Modern organizations, for example, are characterized and impacted by functional and divisional units, vertically integrated strategies, rapid social and technological change, governmental regulation, and resource scarcity, to name a few phenomena. To describe any one of these aspects and to analyze a specific organizational problem in isolation from other influential elements are relatively easy tasks, but the end results will necessarily be fragmented. For instance, although one might understand the strategic decision underlying a more diversified approach to a business activity, the systemic effect of this strategy on the rest of the organization and its elements is much more difficult to evaluate.

The burden for management science has thus been on the development of a more macro-oriented or holistic perspective to delve into these situations and the resulting interactions between (1) the *elements* within the organization and (2) the organization and its environment. Indeed, complex organizations require equally complex modes of inquiry if the processes that occur within them are to be fully understood. One such approach toward building a conceptual scheme for viewing organizations at this appropriate level of complexity has been *systems theory*. Although a complete discussion of systems thought is not necessary for our present purpose and is available in other sources,[6] a brief delineation of an organizational systems model provides a useful context for the analysis of employee attitudes.

The concept of a system suggests that things do not simply happen, but rather that they evolve from multiple pressures entailing multiple outcomes. Discussions of systems in the physical sciences are usually characterized by precise mathematical terms and equations set forth in a causal sequence. By contrast, the complex and multifaceted nature of modern organizations lends itself toward a more qualitative delineation. As such, organizations are referred to as multivariate social systems, composed of at least four basic components: (1) *an administrative or structural configuration*, (2) *a set of tasks* to be performed with a *related technology* or set of tools to accomplish the tasks, (3) *a human or social component* that emerges from organizational activities, and finally (4) *an informational or decision-making subsystem*.[7]

The system is separated from its environment by a permeable boundary. This boundary is somewhat arbitrary and may be

readjusted according to the situation, the degree of interaction between the organization and its environment, or changes in the environment itself. In our recent past, for example, the key strategic
issues for business were thought of almost exclusively in technological and economic terms and the boundary for business planners was
generally drawn around these societal aggregations. With the
emerging complexity of our contemporary environment, however,
reliance solely on economic and technological factors can leave the
organization "exposed" to numerous other pressures and trends.
Thus, as Ian Wilson at General Electric has articulated, the new
planning parameters must include social and political trends and
changes as well as the traditional reliance on economic and technological forecasting. In summary, the environment of business and
the boundaries relevant for analysis have been expanded.[8]

This notion of a boundary further suggests that a system is affected
by certain forces but not by others. Systems that are completely self
contained and do not involve any interaction with the environment
are referred to as *closed systems*. Systems that interact with the
environment and are influenced by outside forces are defined as
open systems. These types are in fact only theoretical possibilities,
because no system is totally open or totally closed. However, the
degree to which a system is closed or open provides a significant
basis for analysis. In the past, for example, many organizations followed a *closed systems strategy* in which the emphasis was placed on
control and the elimination of uncertainty—"fending off" the environment. Effective in certain situations (for instance, where the unit
in question is relatively removed from the environment), a closed
system strategy can have disastrous consequences in other situations
(for example, our automotive industry). An *open systems strategy*,
by contrast, assumes a much more uncertain environment and depends more heavily on scanning and monitoring in strategic planning and development.[9] Thus the organization is ultimately forced to
interact with the environment rather than attempt to isolate itself.

Organizations, of course, are open systems characterized by the
exchange of inputs and outputs with the larger environment. Figure
1–1 presents a basic input-process-output systems model. Each organization receives various inputs from its larger environment,
transforms these factors into an energetic output back to the environment, and receives feedback on its performance. The output of
any given system subsequently becomes the input to some related
system. In a bank, for example, deposits can be perceived as an

Figure 1–1 Elementary Systems Model

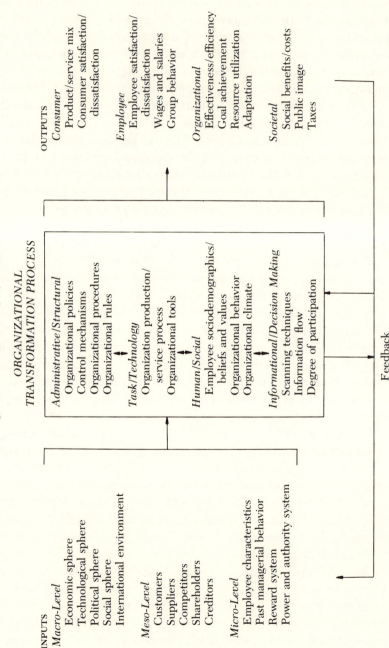

*ORGANIZATIONAL
TRANSFORMATION PROCESS*

INPUTS

Macro-Level
Economic sphere
Technological sphere
Political sphere
Social sphere
International environment

Meso-Level
Customers
Suppliers
Competitors
Shareholders
Creditors

Micro-Level
Employee characteristics
Past managerial behavior
Reward system
Power and authority system

Administrative/Structural
Organizational policies
Control mechanisms
Organizational procedures
Organizational rules

Task/Technology
Organization production/
  service process
Organizational tools

Human/Social
Employee sociodemographics/
  beliefs and values
Organizational behavior
Organizational climate

Informational/Decision Making
Scanning techniques
Information flow
Degree of participation

OUTPUTS

Consumer
Product/service mix
Consumer satisfaction/
  dissatisfaction

Employee
Employee satisfaction/
  dissatisfaction
Wages and salaries
Group behavior

Organizational
Effectiveness/efficiency
Goal achievement
Resource utilization
Adaptation

Societal
Social benefits/costs
Public image
Taxes

Feedback

input that is transformed (through record keeping) into consumer outputs (loans, mortgages, and so forth). As recent fiduciary trends have indicated, however, the banking system is indeed an open one, and many other factors influence this process. Thus organizations receive inputs from the environment, these resources are transformed into usable outputs for their consumers within the confines of the larger environment, and the outputs of one system become the inputs of the related user system.

As shown in Figure 1–1, the administrative/structural subsystem constitutes the core of the organization: task groupings such as units, departments, or divisions; work rules and policies; authority systems such as reporting relationships, power bases, and control procedures; and communication and planning practices and procedures.

The task/technology subsystem consists of the division of work to be accomplished for the organization to complete its end product successfully. Within this sphere, the tools, procedures, and knowledge that enable the product or service to be completed are also considered.

The human or social component is made up by the skills and abilities of the organization's members; the intangibles of these individuals, such as their beliefs, values, and general affect; and their behavior, which emerges in the organization. Since much of this behavior occurs within a group context, the impact of norms, intraorganizational statuses, competition and cooperation, and nonprogrammed activities and interactions must also be considered. Finally, the informational or decision-making component of the organization consists of the processes, techniques, and level and degree of employee involvement in significant decisions. Moreover, the flow of information throughout the organization is another critical aspect.

Clearly, these four subsystems are highly interdependent. Indeed, the way an organization is structured should depend on the type of task to be performed, the available technology, and the volatility of the marketplace. The nature of a given task also places certain constraints on the skills and abilities required of the employee population. Due to the systemic nature of organizations and the interdependency between the component parts, the consistency or "fit" between these subsystems is very important for effective organizational performance.[10] The basic premise underlying this principle is that an organization will operate more effectively and more efficiently when harmony and congruence exist between its parts. Thus, a particular set of tasks will demand a particular organizational configuration, a specific set of skills, and an appropriate decision-making subsystem. The greater the consistency between these aspects of the organization, the greater the probability of success.

Specifically, the fit between any two component parts is defined as the extent to which the needs, demands, goals, objectives, and structures of one component are consistent with the needs, demands, goals, objectives, and structures of another component. A "fit" is thus the mutual consistency between pairs of components.[11] It is hypothesized that organizations with a greater degree of congruence between their component parts are more effective in attaining their goals; therefore, management can improve organizational performance by analyzing their organization's incongruities.

This type of situational or contingency perspective has several implications for business management. Contemporary managers must be able to diagnose the organization adequately, determine the location and nature of inconsistent fits between the component parts, and develop courses of action to raise the degree of consistency without bringing about dysfunctional, latent effects.[12] Looking directly at the fit between the individual and the organization, it becomes apparent that the extent to which an individual's needs and expectations are met by the organizational structure and task influences the employee's satisfaction and commitment to that organization. Indeed, the degree to which individuals hold clear or distorted perceptions of their organization and the degree to which organizations understand how employees feel about their work can play a significant role in the ultimate success or failure of the organization.

The Psychological Contract

The interaction between the individual and the organization is a dynamic, two-way process; both participate only because of what each expects to receive in exchange for involvement in the relationship. This interaction consists of a mutual sense of obligation between the interacting parties, or what is referred to as *reciprocation*. Organizations employ individuals because their services are essential for the organization to achieve its goals successfully. Individuals, in turn, relinquish some of their personal autonomy and independence to the organization in order to fulfill their personal needs. This relationship is cooperative *only* when it offers both entities— the individual and the organization—the opportunity to fulfill their respective needs.[13]

In the field of organizational behavior, this reciprocal relationship has been termed the *psychological contract*. This contract can be defined as the link between the individual and the organization represented by the expectations of each party.[14] Although often articulated by an organization's management, the "contract" is termed psychological because it is largely unwritten and unverbalized. Certain material rewards and benefits are explicitly stipulated and agreed upon, but psychological factors such as job satisfaction, expectations of challenging work, fair treatment, and so forth are more implicit. Moreover, this "psychological income and benefits," although unstated, is perhaps one of the most critical components.

The psychological contract may have both functional and dysfunctional effects on organizational performance. In fact, the kind of contract that develops depends on a number of factors, including the ways organizations treat their members, the various values and norms that operate within organizations, and the type of power base and institutional arrangements utilized by an organization.[15] Etzioni, for example, has developed a typology of this individual-organization relationship by classifying organizations according to the kind of *power and authority structure* they use to elicit compliance and the kind of *involvement* that is subsequently elicited from organizational members.[16] Basically, organizations have three main power bases at their disposal: coercive, utilitarian, and normative. Organizations that utilize a predominantly coercive power base—that is, control through the use of threats and punishment—tend to elicit a type of alienative involvement on the part of their members. Individuals are not truly involved psychologically with the organization and their membership is maintained through force.

The second type of control system is based on rational-legal authority and uses economic rewards and incentives in exchange for membership and performance. This remunerative or utilitarian power base tends to evoke a type of calculative involvement, an extrinsic relationship that is often exemplified by the expression "a fair day's work for a fair day's pay." Finally, organizations that stress a normative power base—that is, the use of symbolic rewards and incentives such as prestige, recognition, and respect—elicit more of a moral commitment from their members. In this situation membership is often an end in itself rather than a means to some other end. Most organizations in the normative sector would be not-for-profit and voluntary organizations.

These three control systems, the levels of involvement they tend to elicit, and the types of psychological contracts that are formulated are summarized in Table 1–1. Although "incongruent," mixed types of contracts are common (for example, a utilitarian-coercive contract, as is characteristic of the armed services); the kind of contract formed depends heavily on the control system employed by the organization. Empirical investigation has further shown the predictive ability of the typology.[17] For example, an organization that primarily uses pay incentives and other economic rewards to motivate and involve its members to perform should expect a calculative type of commitment from its employees. If members are expected to display loyalty to the organization, to be intrinsically motivated in their work, and to be psychologically committed, the organization may be asking its workers to give more than they receive in return. Relating this concept to the notion of "fit" discussed earlier suggests a low degree of congruency between what the organization desires and what the organization actually receives from its members.

The business environment is becoming increasingly complex and, especially in service-related organizations, dependent on high-quality performance from employees throughout the organization —managers and workers alike. Thus organizations must move toward a psychological contract that emphasizes intrinsic motivation.[18] Although business organizations will still rely on a utilitarian power structure as the main basis for their contract, many organizations have begun to move toward the use of control systems

Table 1–1   Types of Psychological Contract, Based on Organizational Control Systems

Type of Involvement	Type of Control System		
	Coercive	Utilitarian	Normative
Alienative	Forced contract		
Calculative		Extrinsic contract	
Moral			Intrinsic contract

SOURCE: Adapted from A. Etzioni, *A Comparative Analysis of Complex Organizations* (Glencoe, Ill.: Free Press, 1961).

with normative overtones. By establishing a "fit" between the needs of the individual and those of the organization, managers can influence a psychological transaction that is beneficial to both parties. [19]

In discussing some of the implications of using a systems model to conceptualize organizations, the need for analysis and diagnosis was stressed. One of the main ways that an organization can begin to gather data on the needs, values, perceptions, and expectations of its employee population is through a carefully constructed survey feedback program. Rather than simply assuming that workers want more opportunity for growth, involvement in organizational decision making, more flexible workdays, or even more money, a survey feedback program enables the organization to pinpoint these factors much more precisely. Such a program has become even more critical in contemporary society when one considers the "fit" between the organization and the larger environment.

The Psychosocial Contract and the New Breed of Worker

The discussion so far has focused on the interrelationships and interdependency of internal organizational components. Since organizations are open systems, however, and are affected by external forces, the consistency between the organizational structure and management style and environmental demands must also be evaluated. For our purposes, we will focus primarily on organizational concerns related to the changing nature and values of the work force.

The same type of contract that links individuals with organizations can be extended to include the larger society. We have explained that the employee and the organization have unwritten and unverbalized assumptions and expectations about each other; the same is true of the organization and society. [20] In forming this macro-level, psychosocial contract, the psychological contract that was discussed earlier has combined with the traditional "social contract" to form a complex pattern of interaction among the individual, the organization, and society. This interaction is a powerful determinant of ultimate organizational success. Not only does the interdependence among these three sectors influence the overall attainment of organizational goals, but it also acts as a mediating influence for dealing with social concerns.

As members of society, employees are one of the links an organization has with the larger environment. Since we are all affected by general social trends, global changes can have an indirect effect on an organization through its members in addition to more direct impacts. For example, expectations and perceptions of quality of life issues that change over time can affect people's work-related expectations and roles.[21] Due to the rising expectations and demands of today's work force, organizations that respond to these societal trends will find that not only are they being responsive to personal needs and social demands, but they are also following good business procedure. Although business organizations have already become more oriented toward the needs of the employee, current trends demonstrate the necessity to continue this concern. Indeed, efforts at establishing more meaningful work, more clearly developed career paths, and, in general, greater flexibility in dealing with employees and their problems are becoming the hallmark of human resource decisions in the 1980s.

As work-related expectations change, many individuals are becoming more active in their demands.[22] Echoing the findings of the government task force report entitled *Work in America*, for example, one of the weekly newsmagazines reported recently on what pollster Daniel Yankelovich has referred to as the "new breed of worker." The article began with this statement: "Never before in our history have American workers been so well paid, so privileged, and yet so discontent in their jobs as they are today."[23] This "new breed" of worker is more highly educated, potentially more mobile in terms of job changes, more demanding of benefits and leisure time, and more affluent than workers of previous generations. Composed of an increasing number of women, minorities, age cohorts, and dual-career families, our labor force itself is also becoming much more diverse sociodemographically than it has ever been before.[24] These factors are interacting with rising expectations and desires for meaningful and challenging work. The diversity of our labor force, combined with changing job-related orientations, thus presents a number of potential problems for business organizations. Indeed, the need to understand these expectations and perceptions fully and the ability to act on them will be an important component of managerial responsibility in the coming decade.

The significance of understanding these attitudes and feelings becomes even more apparent in light of our knowledge of individual behavior. Indeed, the causal relationships between job satisfaction, motivation, performance and perception, and other factors, when added to the mix, make the issues of why people behave in the way they do all the more complex. Only recently have these psychological issues begun to be systematically dissected.

Job Satisfaction and Motivation

Thirty years ago the prevailing assumption was that the higher the job satisfaction, the greater the performance on the job. This assumption, however, was seriously questioned by two researchers who conducted a literature search of satisfaction-performance studies and found quite variable results. Overall, they found almost as many negative correlations with regard to satisfaction and performance as they found positive associations.[25] The uncertainty of this relationship was confirmed in later studies from the 1950s to the 1970s.[26] Thus it could no longer be said with any certainty that high satisfaction leads to high motivation for job performance.

About the same time as the early satisfaction-performance research, various theories of motivation were also becoming popular. In fact, some of these theories remain the basis of many management workshops today. The most widely quoted of these conceptual models is a theory by Abraham Maslow which states that there are five levels of needs, arranged in a hierarchy, and that one must satisfy the lower-level needs before moving on to higher-level needs.[27] Although Maslow has modified his theory, his basic framework has remained unchanged. He hypothesized that the first set of needs that had to be satisfied were physiological in nature, including the need for food and water. All of a person's efforts would be focused on these basic existence needs until they were satisfied. Once these needs were taken care of, the individual would then work toward satisfying the next level of needs. These were referred to as safety needs, such as shelter and security. Once people were in relative safety, their social needs would begin to emerge. Different theorists have referred to these needs as the "need for affiliation"[28] and "relatedness."[29] Next, individuals would be confronted with esteem needs—that is, people had to be involved with activities that recognized them for their contribution to groups, organizations, or others who were significant in their lives. In other motivational models this need has been equated with the need for power.[30] Finally, Maslow suggested that once all of these needs were met people could become concerned about their own development. Maslow called this need "self-actualization," although other theorists termed similar needs "growth"[31] and the "need for achievement."[32] In Maslow's model individuals are thus motivated to fulfill unsatisfied needs in this hierarchical fashion, alternating between needs on the basis of their salience.

Another research-based theory by Fredrick Herzberg, commonly called motivator-hygiene theory, is worth noting, although Herzberg's critics believe his results were determined by his methodology.[33] Herzberg's findings assume that motivation is composed of two factors: (1) those issues and activities that prevent dissatisfaction but do not propel workers to grow and (2) those that actually do motivate workers to grow. These two factors were largely unrelated and were determined by asking workers questions about what made them unhappy or dissatisfied and what made them happy and satisfied. Since there is a cultural bias to attribute one's dissatisfaction to others and one's happiness or accomplishments to oneself, not surprisingly Herzberg found that peripheral issues related to the job—for example, working conditions and supervision—fell into one factor (hygiene), which he linked to job dissatisfaction. In contrast, issues central to the job—for example, the job itself and amount of responsibility—fell largely into the other factor (motivators), which he argued contributed to satisfaction. Although Herzberg's methodology has become suspect, he is credited with providing the field with a new way of looking at worker motivation. A focus solely on hygiene factors could only prevent job dissatisfaction. For workers to be truly satisfied and to perform beyond minimum standards, motivators had to be built into their jobs.

The interrelationships between these different perspectives are presented in Figure 1–2. In sum, all of these theories of motivation provided the blueprint for much of the management and organization development that occurred in the 1960s and 1970s. These theories provided a conceptually simple framework to describe behavior. Since they did not consistently predict behavior, however, social scientists went beyond the content of needs per se to explain human motivation. This new framework, generally referred to as *expectancy theory*, has three components.[34] The first, called *valence*, is the relative importance of an outcome or goal to the individual. Short hours, for instance, may have a moderately high valence for a worker, but a high salary based on longer hours may have a higher valence. An interesting job may have an even higher valence. Since

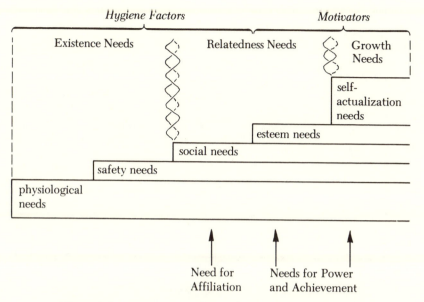

Figure 1-2 Interrelationships Among Motivation Theories.

people are different, the relative importance of certain goals—that is, their valences—can vary considerably. Thus discovering what is important to particular individuals must precede being able to fully motivate them.

The second and third components of expectancy theory are the effort-performance relationship (expectancy) and the performance-outcome relationship (instrumentality). *Expectancy* is the extent to which people subjectively link their behavior to an immediate outcome or goal. *Instrumentality* refers to the subjective link between accomplishing that immediate outcome and the ability to reach other, related goals. Both these relationships can be expressed as probabilities, usually ranging from 0 (low) to 1.00 (high).

Assume for a moment that there is a possibility of a bonus for a group, but this bonus is contingent on preparation of a special report that must be well done and be of value to management. The bonus is important to the people (has a high valence), so they are willing to work hard on the report. However, if the workers are unclear as to the type of report management wants, working hard may be perceived by some as wasting time. Since the effort involved on the report may require additional work hours which cut into household responsibilities, expectations of potential marital problems could

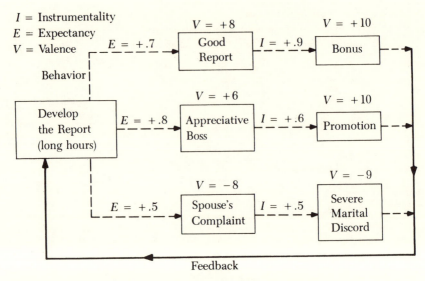

Figure 1-3   Expectancy Motivation Model.

outweigh the bonus, especially if what constitutes a "useful" report is unclear. Thus the probability linking the effort and performance together will be relatively low. Even though it might be acknowledged that a group of employees worked hard on a report (high performance), the report (outcome) may be of high quality (performance), but may not be very helpful to management (low instrumentality). Thus the valent item (the bonus) is in jeopardy for the people who perceived themselves as working hard but in actuality did not produce a product that was useful to the organization (see Figure 1–3).

This conceptualization is important because it reverses the way in which we think about the relationship between motivation and job satisfaction. Originally, satisfaction was thought to precede motivation and performance. More recently it is hypothesized that as high performance is rewarded, the reward leads to high satisfaction.[35] Thus the implication for business focuses on what management can do to ensure high performance, which can lead to highly valent outcomes for the individual and will, in turn, create high satisfaction. Basically, the process is a form of behavioral modification. In other words, if desired behavior is rewarded, productivity will increase and satisfaction should follow. This process can be initiated through a quality of work life survey. Such an effort can examine differing perceptions or role expectations of a job, show how workers and supervisors may differ in their perceptions, provide data for a follow-up group to find ways for workers and supervisors to reconcile these differing role expectations, or even form a basis to make the worker's job more interesting, thus allowing for a more rewarding experience.

Attribution Theory

To further understand workers' behavior, a brief review of attribution theory may be useful.[36] Since the way we analyze a situation determines how we may attempt to solve a problem, a study of attribution theory exposes the *perceived* (but not necessarily actual) causal links between antecedent conditions and factors and subsequent behavior. For instance, if a trainee is not doing well on the job and we think that the poor performance is due to laziness, we will come up with a much different solution than if we think the problem is due to an unclear job description or to the structure of the job itself. According to one brief review of how attribution theory operates,[37] we first observe behavior, or hear about an action, and then determine whether the behavior was intentional or accidental. If the behavior was intentional, we try to assess whether the action was determined by the situation or by the actor's personality. For instance, if behavior for the same employee over different jobs is similar when other employees' behavior differs for each job, we would likely attribute that person's behavior to personality traits instead of to job related characteristics. A number of factors may help us determine why a person acted in a certain way. Our methods for making these determinations, however, are not completely rational; they are referred to as *attributional biases*. For instance, if we think an employee's substandard work is being done to "hurt" us, we may attribute the behavior to personality (spite, anger, prejudice, etc.) rather than situational factors such as not having enough time to do the job well. The point behind this brief discourse on attribution theory is that when we interpret data suggesting that a section of an organization is having difficulty or is demoralized, we must analyze that information in such a way that we do not attribute employees' behavior or attitudes to inappropriate personality or situational factors.

Extrinsic and Intrinsic Rewards

One final distinction in motivation that is closely related to
Herzberg's two-factor theory is the difference between extrinsic and
intrinsic rewards and how these two types of motivation are related
to performance and to satisfaction.[38] *Extrinsic rewards* are the outcomes that come to mind when we think about rewards in
general—pay, fringe benefits, and working conditions are common
examples. *Intrinsic rewards*, on the other hand, are more intangible; they might include growth on the job, esteem, or the interest or
curiosity that a job may offer. Intrinsic rewards are intimately related to the nature of the work, whereas extrinsic rewards are related
to the context and material aspects of the work itself. A Christmas
bonus (extrinsic), for example, may have very little motivating power
because all the employees get one each year whether they have
worked hard or not. The year in which they do not get it may be
because of external economic conditions, not because of job performance. Thus the relationship of work to this type of bonus can be
very tenuous. Another difficulty with extrinsic rewards is that they
can be punishing as well as rewarding. For instance, if people receive a bonus for a good suggestion to management, and then other
workers avoid these people or sabotage their work because they
have violated group norms, the initiators of the ideas have actually
been "punished" for their suggestion.

If a job is intrinsically interesting, heaping extrinsic rewards (for
example, money, benefits, and other perquisites) on the incumbent
may be inappropriate. Research suggests that adding extrinsic rewards to an already intrinsically rewarding job is redundant and does
not necessarily increase an individual's motivation, performance or
satisfaction.

Clearly organizations benefit by offering intrinsically motivating
jobs. Obviously, however, some jobs are very difficult to enrich in
this fashion. Thus, careful thought must be given to such job redesign. One reason for administering a quality of work life survey is to
gain further insight into the performance-reward-satisfaction relationship for particular jobs in particular divisions within an organization. The data obtained by such surveys may or may not be a
surprise, but this information will add substantial credibility to management's attempt to motivate workers.

Summary and Plan of the Book

Worker attitudes have a complex relationship with the on-the-job situation. The feelings, needs, desires, and disappointments of the man or woman on the job both shape and are shaped by the work they do. There is a continual interaction between the skills and attitudes people bring to the work place. Even though job descriptions usually define the parameters of the job, the incumbent truly shapes the job according to his or her feelings and skills.

Work attitudes intertwine with the "psychological contract" discussed earlier. This unwritten set of assumptions is frequently the locus of unfavorable attitudes by workers about their organization since unfavorable attitudes are often due to unfulfilled expectations. The advent of the two-career family, higher education levels, higher amounts of discretionary income, and higher work-related expectations all mean that the dull, boring job of the past is less likely to be tolerated. In the future people will use their new affluence to be more careful in job selection, and many will leave jobs that are unsatisfying. One sector where this pattern already appears to be occurring is in the high technology industry.

On a micro-level, as behavioral scientists and managers become more knowledgeable about the relationship between performance and satisfaction, we will be in a better position to design work so that high performance and feelings of fulfillment are the rule rather than the exception. In order to pinpoint the difficulties on the job and in the organization, however, measuring worker and management attitudes is a critical first step. Assessment of these attitudes thus becomes an appropriate starting point before attempting job redesign or organizational restructure.

Within the preceding context, the remainder of the book focuses on the assessment of the quality of work life through a survey-based approach. Throughout our discussion of the survey feedback process, we will draw principally on two surveys we recently conducted: an ongoing program in a medium-sized savings bank and an initial intervention in a research laboratory. These two efforts will serve as illustrative material to exemplify the problems, pitfalls, and potentialities of survey-guided development programs. Chapter 2 examines the reasons why organizations undertake attitude surveys. Clearly the specific reasons why people feel the way they do about their work situations is important information for an organization to have and to act upon. The chapter continues with a comparison of survey feedback and other attitude data-gathering techniques. Although surveying is the most frequent approach, interviewing, sensing, and observing are among other techniques used in different circumstances.

The Cyclical Planned Intervention Model is a development from three earlier organizational development models: intervention theory, planned change, and action research. (The outline of the book in fact parallels the operation of the Cyclical Planned Intervention Model, which is presented in schematic form in Figure 2–2 on page 47.) The model and its formulation will be fully explained in Chapter 2. Finally, Chapter 2 ends with a brief discussion on the promise of organizational development in changing environmental conditions.

Chapter 3 presents planning and development of the survey. Initial diagnosis is stressed as an important stage, and sufficient time should be allocated for an accurate analysis of an organization's situation. The choice of using internal or external consultants and how organizational entry occurs are also discussed. The chapter presents an outline of how to conduct a preliminary diagnosis of an organization, wherein sensing groups and meetings with personnel officers lead to the development of the survey instrument itself. The chapter closes with a discussion of pitfalls to guard against while developing the survey.

Chapter 4 discusses administrative procedures. In it we attempt to answer the questions with which every survey researcher has to cope, from lead time issues to the development of response forms to the development of instructions and other correspondence. How to prepare the respondents for a survey intervention is also included.

Chapter 5 describes the data analysis phase of survey-guided development programs. Initial treatment of the data, quantitative and qualitative analysis techniques, and interpretation of the survey results are discussed. The chapter ends with a section on organizational feedback and follow-up activities after a survey has been completed.

Chapter 6 presents a final word on organizational surveys, including survey-based organization development efforts, the impact of the external environment on survey results, and the importance of continuity in quality of work life interventions.

Endnotes

1. G. Starling, *The Changing Environment of Business: A Managerial Approach* (Boston: Kent, 1980).
2. E. Vogel, *Japan as Number One: Lessons for America* (Cambridge, Mass.: Harvard University Press, 1979). R.E. Winter, "Multiple Choice: Many Culprits Named in National Slowdown of Productivity Gains," *Wall Street Journal*, October 21, 1980, pp. 1, 24.
3. A. Carroll, "A Three Dimensional Conceptual Model of Corporate Performance," *Academy of Management Review* 4:4(1979), pp. 497–505; H. Tombari, "The New Role of Business Management," *The Collegiate Forum* (Fall 1979), p. 12.
4. L. Preston and J. Post, *Private Management and Public Policy* (Englewood Cliffs, N.J.: Prentice-Hall, 1975); V. Barry, *Moral Issues in Business* (Belmont, Calif.: Wadsworth, 1979).
5. D. Mankin, *Toward a Post-Industrial Psychology: Emerging Perspectives on Technology, Work, Education and Leisure* (New York: Wiley, 1978).
6. L. von Bertalanffy, *General Systems Theory: Foundations, Development, Applications* (New York: Braziller, 1967); L. von Bertalanffy, "The History and Status of General Systems Theory," *Academy of Management Journal* 15:4 (1972), p. 411; C.G. Schoderbek, P.P. Schoderbek, and A.G. Kefalas, *Management Systems: Conceptual Considerations* (Dallas: Business Publications, 1980); D. Katz and R.L. Kahn, *The Social Psychology of Organizations* (New York: Wiley, 1966).
7. P. Hersey and K. Blanchard, *Management of Organizational Behavior: Utilizing Human Resources* (Englewood Cliffs, N.J.: Prentice-Hall, 1977); H.J. Leavitt, "Applied Organizational Change in Industry: Structural, Technical, and Human Approaches," in W.W. Cooper, H.J. Leavitt, and M.W. Shelly, *New Perspectives in Organization Research* (New York: Wiley, 1964); E. Huse and J. Bowditch, *Behavior in Organizations: A Systems Approach to Managing* (Reading, Mass.: Addison-Wesley, 1977).
8. G. Starling, *op. cit.*; E. Mollander, *Responsive Capitalism* (New York: McGraw-Hill, 1980); I. Wilson, "Socio-Political Forecasting: A New Dimension to Strategic Planning," *Michigan Business Review*, July 1974, pp. 14–26.
9. J. Thompson, *Organization in Action* (New York: McGraw-Hill, 1967).
10. D.A. Nadler and M.L. Tushman, "A Diagnostic Model for Organizational Behavior," in J.R. Hackman (ed.), *Perspectives on Behavior in Organizations* (New York: McGraw-Hill, 1977), pp. 85–101; D.A. Nadler and M.L. Tushman, "A Model for Diagnosing Organizational Behavior," *Organizational Dynamics* (Autumn 1980), pp. 35–51.
11. *Ibid.*
12. *Ibid.*
13. E. Schein, *Organizational Psychology* (Englewood Cliffs, N.J.: Prentice-Hall, 1980).
14. K. Thomas, "Managing the Psychological Contract," Intercollegiate Case Clearing House, Harvard Business School Case No. 9-474-159, 1974.
15. E. Schein, *op. cit.*

16. A. Etzioni, *A Comparative Analysis of Complex Organizations* (Glencoe, Ill.: The Free Press, 1961).

17. E. Schein, *op. cit.*; R. Scott, "Job Expectancy—An Important Factor in Labor Turnover," *Personnel Journal* 55:5 (1972), pp. 360–63; E. Huse and J. Bowditch, *op. cit.*

18. E. Schein, *op. cit.*

19. K. Thomas, *op. cit.*

20. L. Nicolaou-Smokovitis, "The Psychosocial Contract: Its Nature and Effects for Greek Industry," *Review of Social Research* 26 (1976) (Athens, Greece: National Center of Social Research).

21. D. Yankelovich, *New Rules: Searching for Self-Fulfillment in a World Turned Upside Down* (New York: Random House, 1981); M. Cooper, B.S. Morgan, P.M. Foley, and L.B. Kaplan, "Changing Employee Values: Deepening Discontent?" *Harvard Business Review* 57:1 (1979), pp. 117–25.

22. D. Yankelovich, *ibid.*; M. Cooper, *et al.*, *ibid.*

23. S. Fritz, "New Breed of Workers," *U.S. News and World Report* (September 3, 1979), pp. 35–38.

24. D.Q. Mills, "Human Resources in the 1980's," *Harvard Business Review* 57:4 (1980), pp. 154–63.

25. A.H. Brayfield and W.H. Crockett, "Employee Attitudes and Employee Performance," *Psychological Bulletin* 52 (1955), pp. 396–424.

26. F. Herzberg, B. Mausner, R.O. Peterson, and D.F. Capwell, *Job Attitudes: Review of Research Opinion* (Pittsburgh: Psychological Series of Pittsburgh, 1957); V. Vroom, *Work and Motivation* (New York: Wiley, 1946); L.W. Porter and R.M. Steers, "Organizational Work and Personal Factors in Employee Turnover and Absenteeism," *Psychological Bulletin* 80 (1973), pp. 151–76.

27. A. Maslow, *Motivation and Personality* (New York: Harper and Brothers, 1954), p. 13.

28. S. Schacter, *The Psychology of Affiliation* (Stanford, Calif.: Stanford University Press, 1959).

29. C.P. Alderfer, "An Empirical Test of a New Theory of Human Needs," *Organizational Behavior and Human Performance* 4:2 (1969), pp. 142–75.

30. A. Adler, *Individual Psychology*, translated by S. Langer, in C. Murchison (ed.), *Psychologies of 1930* (Worcester, Mass.: Clark University Press).

31. Alderfer, *op. cit.*

32. D. McClelland, *The Achieving Society* (Princeton, N.J.: Van Nostrand, 1961).

33. F. Herzberg, B. Mausner, and B. Snyderman, *The Motivation to Work*, 2d ed. (New York: Wiley, 1959).

34. Vroom, *op. cit.*

35. E.E. Lawler and L.W. Porter, "The Effect of Performance on Job Satisfaction," *Industrial Relations* 7 (1967), pp. 20–28.

36. J.M. Bartunek, "Attribution Theory: Some Implications for Organizations," in J.M. Bartunek and J.R. Gordon, *Behavior in Organizations: A Diagnostic Approach* (Lexington, Mass.: Ginn, 1979), pp. 69–74.

37. *Ibid.*

38. B.M. Staw, *Intrinsic and Extrinsic Motivation* (Morristown, N.J.: Silver Burdett Co., 1976).

Chapter 2

SURVEY FEEDBACK AS A MEANS FOR ORGANIZATIONAL CHANGE

Today's work environment is increasingly characterized by rapid and often turbulent change. As a consequence, one of the contemporary manager's most difficult tasks is to successfully initiate and implement various policies and programs that deal with these new situations. Obviously, this goal requires a higher level of sensitivity to what is happening in an organization's environment than was necessary in previous decades. Without such knowledge, the ability of any programs, procedures, or other mechanisms to meet these challenges will be greatly reduced.

This perspective is especially relevant to the stance and orientation of our present generation of workers. As indicated in Chapter 1, the worker of the 1980s is not the same employee who labored in our economic system in earlier decades. The present-day individual's background, motivational requirements, expectations, and perceptions are quite different compared to those of earlier generations.[1] In many instances, however, today's employee is still confronted with the same work structure and methods that characterized our more traditional, industrial work efforts.

The burden placed on managers today is increasingly oriented not only toward understanding the technical aspects of work and the work place, but to discerning and confronting the social perceptions, aspirations, and expectations of the work force as well. Unless managers can accurately perceive the climate or atmosphere that permeates their organizations, many problems will arise or continue. Indeed, this perceptive insight is often the difference between the ultimate success or failure of discretionary managerial decisions—

either corrective actions or the continued misdiagnosis of the problem or situation confronting the organization. If valid information about organizational climates can be gathered, managers will have a firmer basis for understanding and consequently for solving recurring (and nonrecurring) organizational problems.

Within this context, this chapter examines some of the reasons why organizations undertake assessments of quality of work life. Survey feedback—its strengths and weaknesses—is compared to other organizational data-gathering techniques. Our approach, based on the Cyclical Planned Intervention Model (the organizing theme for the rest of the book), is compared to some of the other organizational intervention approaches. Finally, there is a brief discussion on the promise of organizational change.

Reasons for Assessing the Quality of Work Life

In Chapter 1 "quality of work life" issues were referred to as a major theme of human resource decisions in the 1980s. The importance of workers as resources of organizations is further reflected in our recent preoccupation with foreign managerial styles. For example, the current emphasis on the art of Japanese management—whether in terms of "Theory Z"[2] or as "master managers"[3]—points to the ways in which the Japanese business system has focused on the needs and expectations of its employee population. However, in contrast to North American culture, Japanese society is relatively closed and homogeneous. Their tradition of lifetime employment, under which the employer has a responsibility for looking after the worker's general welfare and personal needs,[4] and their reluctance to accept our early principles of Taylorism (or scientific management, as it is often termed[5]) are deeply rooted in both their business world and in their very cultural base. Thus, to a large degree, the subjective orientations of the Japanese labor force are relatively uniform and favorable toward the organizations for which they work. (This favorability in attitudes is further ensured through their performance appraisal system. Employee evaluations in Japanese companies include not only performance measures but also desirable personality traits and behaviors. In fact, in most organizations in Japan personality and behavior, rather than output per se, are the key evaluation criteria. Since each employee is compared along these criteria with other members of an appropriate group and ranked accordingly, there is a clear discriminatory bias which would not be accepted in the United States.)[6]

In a more diverse, pluralistic society such as the United States, the global focus on employee attitudes and values can be a more difficult task. Rather than being homogeneous and closed, our society is characterized more fully by its heterogeneity and openness. As such, the monitoring and evaluation of potentially wide-ranging employee attitudes can be a complex process entailing more extensive efforts than those apparent in Japan. Yet, in spite of the greater range of attitudes in the American work force, measures that have been designed to tap the diligence of American and Japanese workers found orientations which are remarkably similar.[7] Moreover, the success of some Japanese firms that are operating in the United States—most notably SONY in California and Sharp in Tennessee —points out the potential that such efforts focused on the development of people as resources and the quality of their work life can have in the American work place.

Even considering the heterogeneity and diversity of opinion that exist in our society, research has suggested a number of themes or issues that fall under the general rubric of "quality of work life." Briefly, the range of issues involved entails objective appraisals and subjective feelings about such areas as the following:[8]

- Adequate and fair compensation
- Safe and healthy working conditions
- Opportunities to use and develop personal capabilities
- Opportunity for continued growth and security
- Social integration in the work organization (e.g., freedom from prejudice, egalitarianism, support systems, etc.)
- Constitutionalism in the work place (e.g., personal privacy, freedom of speech, due process, etc.)
- Work and total life space (e.g., psychological and social costs of transfers, work loads, etc.)
- Social relevance of work to life

This brief listing of areas included in discussions about the quality of working life begins to suggest the wide range of issues that have become important. Given the diversity and difficulty of these areas, maintaining an understanding of their present and potential impact on employees is no easy task. Subsequently, the consistent monitoring of employee attitudes and opinions has become vital in today's business world.

One of the most widely used approaches to generating systematic and comparative information about how employees feel about different issues is the application of organizational surveys through a process referred to as *survey feedback*. Essentially, survey feedback consists of the collection of data from a specific work unit or the total organization through the use of a structured questionnaire. The data generated from this questionnaire are first summarized, then fed back to the involved workers through reports and workshops, and finally used by the different groups and managers to confront existing and potential organizational problems. In addition, the findings are useful in developing various plans of action from strategic planning to organizational problem solving. As one of the major historical stems in organizational development, survey feedback has proven to be a powerful tool, both in measuring trends in employee perceptions and in improving organizational performance.[9]

Within this context, there are four basic reasons why organizations gather information on employee attitudes and opinions about work and work-related policies and conditions: (1) to facilitate feedback and decision making, (2) to diagnose organizational problems, (3) to improve communication, and (4) to aid in managerial training.[10]

Feedback and Decision Making

Much of the traditional emphasis on the use of feedback in organizations has focused on the performance and education of employees.[11] While these are highly beneficial uses of this information, such data can also provide management with more in-depth knowledge about its own functioning and processes. Especially in larger, decentralized organizations, extensive data-gathering efforts assess how various policies are being accepted by the work force and how effectively they are being implemented.[12] Monitoring employee feelings about quality of work life issues, for example, can provide a more concrete basis for organizational planning and development. Use of such feedback can reduce some of the uncertainty and ambiguity in managerial decision making, especially if the information is gathered in a systematic and comprehensive manner.

In one of the surveys we conducted for a savings bank, employees' feelings about the bank's internal transfer systems led to a restructuring of organizational policies concerning temporary teller transfer from one branch to another. Similarly, a general understanding of worker attitudes about a particular job, a reward or incentive system, or an overall organizational policy can help managers to initiate necessary changes effectively.

Feedback from workers to management can also provide useful insights about the impact of organizational change on the firm's work force. In one of our surveys, for instance, we found that the bank had recently adopted a divisionalized structure to offset its steady increase in size. Based on the input from a subsequent attitude survey, the organization was able to assess how the divisional reorganization was working and what was required to increase its effectiveness.

Diagnosis of Organizational Problems

Another basic function of organizational surveys is to diagnose different problems with which a firm might be confronted. In the development of the systems model of an organization in Chapter 1, we discussed the concept of a "fit" between the components in any group or organization.[13] The main advantage of this framework is that it provides us with a useful way of looking at organizational problems—that is, as inconsistent fits between the different components (people, task, structure, and technology/decision making). The model stressed the importance of data gathering as a key part of the process of diagnosing the degree of fit between the different subsystems. Data that are gathered systematically can help to explain such organizational problems as turnover and absenteeism or even to predict critical events (for example, a threat of job action). Obviously, understanding the causes of these occurrences can enable a firm to minimize potential problems; managers should therefore pay attention to changes in such employee attitudes.

The use of information generated from attitude surveys for diagnostic purposes can range from the mundane to the complex. In one of our surveys for a research laboratory, for example, a major criticism from many of the administrative support personnel stemmed from dissatisfaction with specific working conditions, such as cleanliness in the lavatories, outdated office equipment, and a lack of support from various service-oriented departments. These complaints, of course, are relatively easily rectified. Often the most difficult part of working through such issues is their initial identification.

In other instances, however, the data might not lend themselves as readily to quick "solutions." In these situations the complexity of the particular issue in question can demand the interaction of management and employees to reach a suitable outcome. In one of our bank surveys, the data indicated a fairly uniform dissatisfaction among branch managers and head tellers concerning the relative effectiveness of new tellers assigned to their branches. Based on an analysis of several different questions and open-ended responses from the survey, a number of problems and shortcomings in the teller training program were identified. Using this information, the vice president of personnel appointed a training and development officer to oversee the improvement of teller and other training programs. This person then used the data accumulated from the survey and met with small groups of tellers and branch managers to devise training programs aimed particularly at facilitating the tellers' transition from training to actual customer service. This entire process was somewhat lengthy and, in contrast to the above example, entailed the input of both management and employees to reach a satisfactory outcome.

Communication

Survey feedback programs can provide a useful way to establish an ongoing, two-way communication system between workers and management. As discussed in the earlier section on the use of such data as feedback to management, a major function of organizational surveys is to open the lines of communication—not only in terms of downward communication of company policies to employees, but also to provide an outlet for employees to express their feelings to management. Surveys should provide anonymity to individuals and confidentiality is strictly enforced in most survey procedures. As a result, workers are usually more willing to express their true feelings about different issues—particularly about sensitive ones—than when they fear they could be directly identified.

The two-way communication that can emerge from a survey feedback program can lead to a proactive approach to organizational problem solving as well. During feedback sessions employees are encouraged to discuss the results of the surveys and implications of various issues with the managers involved. Similar to the workings of the Japanese "quality circle," where workers and management come together to discuss and solve organizational problems,* these feed-

---

* In Japan, workers are encouraged to submit their ideas of ways in which the company's products or services might be improved. To facilitate this sharing of information, quality circles are employed, in which people who work together meet

back sessions can serve to improve communication flow through the different levels in the organization. They allow smaller problems to surface *before* they become major issues.

As part of the communication function, the data generated through organizational surveys can also be useful in establishing a precedent for change. Since change is most likely to occur in organizational settings in which individuals feel that new ideas are welcomed and even expected, such data can be used to "unfreeze" existing norms and attitudes.[14] Especially when this information is perceived as valid, accurate, and unbiased, the resulting description of organizational conditions can be a potent force in helping to bring about needed change.

Training

The last main usage of organizational surveys entails the training and development of individual managers. Although this function is probably the most overlooked,[16] the involvement of managers in the survey process can provide both an enlightening experience and a way of developing their abilities in perceiving the more intangible aspects of organizational behaviors. This aspect of surveys exists on a number of different levels.

Most organizations that use surveys employ external consultants to oversee the process and to ensure confidentiality. Additionally, in many instances managers and staff from the personnel department are also included in the process. Their involvement will be discussed more fully later in the chapter. The point here is that such involvement can give managers experience in (1) formulating questions, (2) probing critical situations for a fuller understanding of cause-effect relationships, and (3) developing ways of effectively working with their employees.

From the overall perspective of the organization, the involvement of these individuals can also add a critical dimension to the survey itself. Since many mid-level managers have insights into specific

---

with their foreman/manager. Interestingly, the concept of "quality circles" was introduced to the Japanese in the '50s and '60s by three Americans—Edward Deming and Joseph Juran of New York University and A.V. Feigenbaum of General Electric. Since then, quality circles have become so popular and effective in Japan that estimates are that over 1 million quality circle groups in Japanese industry now involve over 10 million workers. Moreover, the popularity of these groups has spread to other industrialized countries, including a "reintroduction" in the United States, with promising results.[15]

aspects of a firm's operations, they can often facilitate the entry of outside consultants. This interaction not only aids in pinpointing meaningful questions for a particular organization, but also further involves managers and staff in the process of formulating the questions and format of the survey. Moreover, it provides managers the opportunity to raise specific questions and issues with the consultants.

Another use of attitude surveys as a training mechanism is during the feedback or follow-up phase. Since organizations obviously will want to utilize the survey information, managers and employees are often involved in the discussion process, in interpreting the results (usually with the consultants operating as resources), and in devising programs that will further help solve the problems that are identified. The great majority of individuals we have worked with on such surveys seem to feel that the time and effort spent in the process is a valuable learning experience, both in terms of specific aspects of organizational functioning and in more general insights into personal, interpersonal, and group behavior.

Survey Feedback Versus Other Data-Gathering Techniques

Although this book focuses on the use of surveys in organizations, there are a number of different approaches to collecting information about employee attitudes and behaviors. Since many different types of data can be gathered, obviously the most effective method depends on the nature of the problem confronting the organization. Each of these approaches, as we shall see, has its own strengths and weaknesses. Conceptually, these methods can be placed on a continuum in terms of varying degrees of directness in the data-gathering process, the amount of structure they provide, time involved in the process, and applicability to certain types of organizational situations.[17] For convenience, these different techniques are summarized in Table 2–1. To ensure a systematic understanding of these different methods and the basis for selecting the best one, however, it is necessary to review briefly the various types of data-gathering techniques that are available.

The following basic methods are employed in the gathering of data and preliminary diagnosis of organizational situations:[18]

- Questionnaires and instruments
- Interviewing
- Organizational sensing
- Polling
- Observation
- Unobtrusive measures
- Collages and drawings

Questionnaires and Instruments

Survey questionnaires are probably the most widely used of all data-gathering techniques in contemporary society. In addition to being employed in the business world, such questionnaires are the prime method of amassing large amounts of data on public opinions about a wide range of social and political issues. Surveys are particularly useful for studies of the attitudes, beliefs, and values of a particular population. Moreover, they can also provide useful information on changes in these subjective orientations. One of the main strengths of this approach is that the data lend themselves to rigorous, statistical analysis, which can aid in analyzing trends in various situations.

Such questionnaires, however, have a number of potential weaknesses, which, if not carefully considered, can precipitate results that may be only minimally useful. For example, individual questions must be formulated with caution so that respondents are not misled in their answers. Since questionnaires are also somewhat impersonal, in many instances the surveyor is confronted with the problem of nonresponse, in which individuals (for explicit or implicit reasons not always fully understood) choose not to answer specific or large blocks of questions. Since the survey is conducted in an autonomous and private manner, there is usually no way that this information can be updated or probed more fully. As a consequence, a large nonresponse to any particular issue can readily bias the information that is gathered and leave the researcher without recourse.

Various other issues are also important to consider. Quite simply, does the question actually measure what it purports to measure? In many instances questions do not generate the types of data that were initially desired. Moreover, the questions may not tap the responses reliably or consistently. Surveys also require a fairly high degree of trust on the part of the respondent. If the individual involved sus-

Table 2–1 Comparison of Data-Gathering Methods

Method	Characteristics	Main Strengths	Main Weaknesses	Structure	Time Involved	Directness
Survey Questionnaires	Most widely used technique to obtain information from a large number of employees	Particularly useful for studies of beliefs, attitudes, values; data lend themselves to quantitative analysis	Impersonal, problems of nonresponse, question validity, misleading questions	Closed-ended: high Open-ended: low	Relatively economical	Relatively indirect
Survey Instruments	Similar to questionnaires but developed around a specific theme or body of theory; preplanned orientation	Validity, pretested	Likely to miss important issues for a particular organization	High	Economical	Relatively indirect
Interviewing	Questions posed directly to employees	Subjective data can be clarified; more in-depth data can be obtained; greater flexibility and deviation than above two methods	Expensive, requires highly skilled interviewers, difficulty ensuring comparability of data, self-report bias	Closed-ended: moderately high Open-ended: low	Lengthy	Highly direct

Organization Sensing	Unstructured group interviews, usually with a cross section of employees; can involve managers or third-party moderators	Group interaction can lead to "richer" ideas, more thoughtful analysis	High dependence on trust, effective listening skills; low degree of statistical rigor	Low	More economical than personal interview	Highly direct
Polling	Questioning a particular work group about a certain issue, problem	Since whole group takes part, can lead to increased sense of involvement	Does not lend itself to large groups; not scientific	Low to moderate	Short time span	Direct
Observation	Watching actual behavior of people at work, interacting with each other	Flexibility, insights into working arrangements, collection of data on behavior not reports of behavior	Open to perceptual bias, Hawthorne effect, requires highly trained individuals, sampling problems	Casual to highly structured	Varies	Relatively direct
Unobtrusive Measures	Use of records, such as turnover, absenteeism, and production statistics	Uncontaminated data (no respondent bias)	Measures must be used in their proper context and often must be refined, interpretational coding	High	Varies	Highly indirect
Collages and Drawings	Individuals, subgroups, or groups are asked to do a drawing around a particular theme	Nonverbal way of expressing feelings about an issue, situation, etc.	Often perceived as "child's play," difficult to interpret	Low	Moderate time span	Relatively indirect

pects that he or she can be identified in any way, or if the data may be used in a punitive fashion, people will often choose to tell an organization's management what they feel it wants to hear. Consequently, true thoughts about a particular issue remain unexpressed.

Thus, although such surveys are relatively economical, a number of pitfalls must be considered. In addition to those briefly mentioned above, the surveyor must also consider (1) sampling issues, (2) the impact of different types of response sets on how people answer the questions (for example, social desirability, yea-sayers versus nay-sayers, and so forth), (3) processing or coding errors that needlessly distort the data, and (4) errors of causal interpretation. These issues will be examined more extensively in Chapters 3 and 5.

Survey instruments are quite similar to questionnaires except that they are preplanned and developed around specific theoretical bases or ideas. Instruments from such research-based institutes as the Institute for Social Research (ISR) at the University of Michigan, the Cornell Job Description Index (JDI), the Minnesota Satisfaction Questionnaire (MSQ), and the Index of Organizational Reactions (IOR) are examples of this approach.[19] Since these instruments are prepackaged and based on a theoretical framework, they usually have been through a validity-testing process. Thus, there is a greater degree of confidence that the questions are generating data about the specific issues on which they are focused. However, since they are prepackaged, questions sometimes miss issues important for a particular organization and emphasize others that are in fact minor. Research has indicated, for example, that although such "canned" instruments can be highly efficient, surveys that reflect familiarity with key issues for a particular organization seem to achieve better information in terms of both quality and quantity.[20]

Interviewing

Personal interviews are another approach to collecting information about how an organization's employees feel about certain issues and problems. This approach is more direct than the use of questionnaires and canned instruments and can lend deeper insight into the actual meanings of subjective data. Since the face-to-face situation provides greater flexibility and deviation than the survey method, employees can be probed more fully about their attitudes and opinions about a given issue, which can often clarify causal relationships.

Successful interviews, however, require highly skilled interviewers and relatively large amounts of time to probe fully pertinent aspects of the situation. It is not uncommon, for example, for an interview with one individual to approach a full hour in duration. Actually, unskilled interviewers operating in relatively short time spans can do more harm than good in probing an organizational problem.

The degree of structure involved in interviewing can range from relatively open-ended types of questions to highly structured, formalized questions similar to those included in surveys. Even for the more structured questions, however, ensuring comparability of data across individuals is often difficult, especially when a number of different interviewers are employed. Thus, although the interview is highly direct and can produce more in-depth information, it is also a time-consuming and expensive process which often generates data that are not valid for comparative purposes. Consequently, the interview may be extremely useful for pilot data gathering, but for large-scale collection it is seldom feasible.

Organizational Sensing

Organizational sensing is a relatively new approach to gathering information from employees. It is largely characterized by a relatively unstructured group discussion and interview, usually with a cross section of organizational members. This diagonal slice can provide the firm with a valuable data base, for it represents a number of different job categories and levels in the organization and thus varying organizational perspectives. The customary procedure is to form groups from persons who have no direct reporting relationship with each other. Through the interaction that occurs within these sensing groups, individuals often act as catalysts to other group members, and the process frequently results in a richer and more thoughtful analysis of the organization's problems.

Sensing sessions are usually moderated by managers themselves or an independent third party. Each approach has its strengths and weaknesses. With a member of the organization's management leading the session, care must be taken to ensure that a high level of trust and openness exists. Since the quality of data generated by this discussion is greatly influenced by the degree to which people feel comfortable expressing their opinions about a particular subject, any hesitation on the part of those involved can readily distort the resulting information. Third-party moderators can encourage respondents to be more open and truthful in their replies because of their neutrality and greater objectivity. The main disadvantage is that these individuals often do not possess sufficient in-depth information about the organization to fully probe a given issue and ensure that enough critical data have been gathered to analyze the problem adequately.

Sensing sessions are usually unstructured, and the direction they take very much depends on the types of issues the participants are willing to discuss. This approach to data generation is highly direct and is more economical than personal interviews. Moreover, participants experience an increased sense of involvement in the process. Such sessions, however, seem to be most successful when the number of employees involved is relatively small (approximately twenty to thirty). Although highly sensitive information can be gathered in these sessions, the degree of statistical rigor is low, and the quality of the data depends heavily on the listening skills of the moderator.

Polling

Another approach similar to the use of sensing groups is polling. Rather than taking a cross section of employees, polling focuses on a particular work group. The main theme is how the group feels about a certain issue or set of issues. With the current emphasis on productivity, for example, many managers have polled the groups they oversee as to how they feel they could be more effective in their work. This is usually accomplished through the use of nondirective, open-ended questions that are reinterpreted by the groups and discussed by the members. Since the whole group takes part in this process, all the members can experience an increased sense of involvement and participation in the resulting decisions. Polling is quite a direct and simple way of gathering information quickly concerning a particular issue. Conceptually, polling is quite similar to the use of quality circles, although with the latter, the experience is more systematic and consistent in nature.

The main problem with polling is its limited use. Since it does not lend itself to large groups and large issues, it does not provide a general overview of the climate of the organization. Moreover, the questions that guide the discussion are not usually as carefully prepared as those used in professionally developed surveys and thus can result in biased data.

Observations

One of the most effective ways of discovering how work is actually accomplished in a given group is to watch people's behavior as they work or interact with others. Such observations can range from casual, informal perusals of the work process to highly structured ones that use a formal chart to outline specific activities and behaviors. The major strength of this approach is its flexibility and directness. Four varieties of observational roles can be utilized.[21]

Complete Participant.   In this situation the observer joins the group and never makes his or her identity known. An individual, for example, may choose to work in a factory to learn about the inner workings of informal groups. Role-pretense is a major theme—that is, the observer pretends to be a colleague of those in the group being observed. Obviously, this particular role presents a number of ethical dilemmas. Moreover, complete participation can often result in an initially impartial observer's becoming too involved in the particular situation to maintain dispassionate analysis.

Participant-as-Observer.   This observational role is the most common. The observer makes his or her presence known but attempts as fully as possible to become a typical group member. Since the members of the group being observed are aware of the researcher, fewer ethical problems are involved. However, once people know they are being observed, they usually alter their behavior accordingly and thus may present a distorted view of what "normally" happens.*

---

* This bias can be quite pervasive in organizational research. For example, in a series of productivity studies in Western Electric's Hawthorne, Illinois, plant during the late 1920s and early 1930s, researchers decided that their very presence and observations of a group of women who assembled telephone equipment had a major effect on their work behavior. Initially, the research was focused on testing the impact of working conditions on work group output. The researchers found that *regardless* of how they varied the conditions of work, with each major change there was a substantial increase in production. Rather than being attributable to the changes in the working conditions per se, the researchers found that the employees involved perceived themselves to be "special" due to the attention they were receiving from the researchers and management. The women felt that since they were singled out for this research role the organization's management obviously felt that they were important. Not wanting to disappoint either the researchers or the managers, every time one of the experimental variables (lighting, length of rest breaks, free lunches, and so on) was manipulated they worked harder. As a result of this research, the phenomenon of working harder because of the feeling of importance or being observed is referred to as the "Hawthorne effect." Although the pervasiveness of this effect has recently been questioned, it is still generally accepted that our physical presence has a direct effect on the behavior of those around us.[22]

Observer-as-Participant.   This observation method, usually characterized by a one-visit type of interview, encompasses relatively more formal observations than the above two methods. Because the contact is comparatively brief, however, the observer-as-participant is more likely than in the above two methods to misunderstand and be misunderstood by the informant. Thus, brief encounters can often contribute to misperceptions that can set up communication barriers the observer may not be aware of until it is too late.

Complete Observer.   This role entirely removes the observer from any social interaction with informants. The observer attempts to observe others in ways that make it unnecessary for the people involved to take the interviewer into account because the people are not aware of the process. The best example of this type of observation is illustrated by systematic eavesdropping or covert reconnaissance of a work group's activities. As in the complete participant role, complete observation raises a number of ethical dilemmas.

All four observational roles are open to several perceptual biases. Since what we view is influenced by our own subjective feelings and experiences, we often distort the reality. Ask any group of people who have just witnessed a given event, for example, to explain what has taken place. If ten people are present, quite likely you will receive ten different descriptions of what has occurred. In fact, the power of our own perceptual sets is so great that we often do not realize that we are actually creating new meanings for behavior that is not consistent with the reality of the situation. Thus, to be truly effective, observers should be highly trained and skilled.

Unobtrusive Measures

The most indirect form of data collection of the approaches discussed is through the use of unobtrusive measures of organizational happenings. (A particularly well-done compendium of unobtrusive measures, contained in a book appropriately entitled *Unobtrusive Measures,* by E.J. Webb *et al.*,[23] has inspired much of the work done on the subject.) Use of various records such as turnover rates, absenteeism reports, and changes in productivity statistics can often pinpoint potential problems in an organization. Unfortunately, these measures, which are often generated for one purpose, are misleading if they are analyzed out of context. Thus, they should not be taken at face value; rather these measures must be refined and viewed in the appropriate situational context if valid data are to be gained.

Collages and Drawings

One of the least frequently used approaches to gathering information about employee feelings and attitudes is through the utilization of collages or drawings about a specific issue. The process is characterized by asking an individual, subgroup, or group to draw a picture around a particular theme. This might be how they view their work situation or how they depict the people they work with. Its main strength as a data gathering tool is that it can be an effective way for people to express their feelings about a situation in a nonverbal manner. Many studies have indicated, for example, that while managers tend to be highly verbal, often employees at lower levels are less vocal and have more difficulty in expressing how they feel through words.[24] The collage approach thus gives these individuals a greater opportunity for more open expression.

Unfortunately, this method is often viewed as "child's play," and in many instances employees do not take the process seriously. In addition, creating such drawings takes time, and the probability of distorting their interpretation is quite high.

Table 2–1 (pages 32–33) summarizes the characteristics, strengths and weaknesses, structure, time involved, and directness of the data-gathering methods just described. Because each of the various approaches has potential weaknesses, the most effective information collection processes encompass a combination of these methods. Indeed, the most successful attempts at diagnosing organizational problems come from an eclectic use of complementary techniques.

Survey Feedback Programs: The Cyclical Planned Intervention Model

There are a number of different approaches to organizational feedback programs, but the one we have found most useful integrates the different theories of organizational change and provides a practitioner-oriented framework. Three basic models of change have been popularized in the literature: intervention theory, planned change, and action research. Each of these will be discussed briefly to set the foundation for the survey feedback model we propose.

Intervention Theory

Developed by Chris Argyris, intervention theory and methodology are based on the concept that organizations by themselves, without help, do not know how to generate sufficient information relevant to the specific problems they are confronting.[25] Consequently, organizations are unable to use that information to develop alternative solutions, or to make decisions and develop an organizational commitment to those decisions that is shared throughout the firm. The assumption is made, however, that the organization can improve by (1) diagnosing inadequate processes and (2) establishing corrective actions to make those processes more effective through a series of *interventions.* *

The strategy of intervention theory revolves around three basic criteria:

1. The organization is assisted in generating explicit and verifiable information about its various work processes. These data are focused on the firm as a whole rather than any particular subgroup or individual. Of course, in systems theory this focus may be on a specific subsystem that can be considered a system in its own right.

2. The organization must have a free choice among the alternative courses of action. Based on the information gathered in the initial phase, final decision making is placed with the organization's management rather than with external or internal consultants. This component is important to ensure an organizational commitment to the course of action chosen and to minimize dependence on the consultant.

3. Finally, the organization must also have a high degree of ownership of the alternative selected. Essentially, this means that the managers involved have "internalized" the data and perceive that the action involved fulfills the needs, values, and objectives of the different levels of the system (individual, group, and organizational).

---

* Interventions are usually defined as "sets of structured activities in which selected organizational units (target groups or individuals) engage with a task or a sequence of tasks where the task goals are related directly or indirectly to organizational improvement." These interventions can be achieved through an external consultant, an internal consultant, or a joint collaboration between a consultant and the client organization.[26]

Thus, the role of the consultant (often referred to as an interven-tionist) is to try to alter the basic processes of information flow, data gathering, and decision making within the organization rather than to make specific suggestions for change per se.[27]

Planned Change

A second approach to generating change in organizations is through a planned change model. Even though this model has been continu-ally redeveloped and refined, it essentially entails two basic princi-ples: (1) all information must be freely and openly shared between the organization's management and the consultant (often referred to as a change agent) and (2) such information is helpful only when it is translated into action.[28] The underlying concept is a seven-step, dynamic process:[29]

1. *Scouting:* joint exploration of the organizational situation by consultant and management;
2. *Entry:* mutual development of a contract and expectations by the consultant and the organization;
3. *Diagnosis:* identification of specific goals for improvement;
4. *Planning:* identification of plan of action and potential resis-tance to planned changes;
5. *Action:* actual implementation of plan of action;
6. *Evaluation:* assessment of the success of the change program and determination of the need for further actions or termina-tion;
7. *Termination:* end of the particular change project; consultant either leaves the organization or moves on to a different project.

Thus, the basis of planned change is oriented toward conscious and deliberate efforts to improve a particular organizational system.[30] The actual process by which such attempts are implemented can be divided into the following three basic strategies.[31]

Empirical-Rational. This strategy assumes that the individuals involved are rational and that they will follow their self-interests once they are revealed to them. Essentially straightforward and uncomplicated, this intervention is based on the concept that when a change is desirable, and in the self-interest of the individual or group involved, the proposed change will be accepted if its under-lying logic can be effectively communicated.

Normative–Re-educative.   This strategy is based on the assumption that behavior is guided by social and cultural norms and the degree of commitment to these norms. As a result, change is not always accepted on a rational basis but rather is often influenced by more personalized and intangible variables (for example, values, attitudes, habits, and so on). Thus, change programs should be based not on logical reasoning per se, but rather on the involvement and collaboration of those taking part in the change process.

Power-Coercive.   The third strategy is based on the assumption that individuals with less power usually comply with those individuals with more power. Power is often defined as the ability to exert influence. Within organizations this can be viewed as the ability to make things happen and to get things accomplished.[32] French and Raven have delineated five different types of power: (1) *legitimate*, based on the individual's position or status in the organization; (2) *expert*, based on the degree of authority or knowledge; (3) *referent*, also referred to as charismatic power based on the person's attractiveness to others; (4) *reward*, based on the individual's ability to reward cooperative behavior; and (5) *coercive*, the ability to punish uncooperative behavior.[33]*

Empirical-rational strategies are based on a sharing of expert power (knowledge of the particular situation). Similarly, normative–re-educative strategies are based on a sharing of expertise about human behavior. Power-coercive strategies, by contrast, are not based on such sharing, but rather on the explicit use of power through either nonviolence (for example, consumer boycotts and civil rights), invocation of political institutions (for example, government regulation), or manipulation.[35] Manipulation, however, poses a potential problem with power-coercive strategies in that those affected often view such strategies as illegitimate. This can have a long-term, dysfunctional impact on the organization.

Action Research

Similar to the dynamic process underlying planned change, the action research model refers to a cycle of data-based problem solving

---

* Another way of looking at power is as a dependent variable—that is, it is caused by particular organizational attributes. Individuals, group, or subunits within an organization will have more power if (1) they cope with more uncertainty than others, (2) they are more central to the operation of the organization, (3) they are less easily replaced, and (4) they work at less routine tasks. In short, the more unique, but central, the subunit is to the organization, the more power it will have.[34]

that replicates the process of scientific inquiry. In fact, action research is both a process (i.e., an ongoing series of events and actions)
as well as an approach to organizational problem solving.[36] Action
research involves a constantly unfolding, iterative interplay among
diagnosis, solutions, results, rediagnosis, and new solutions to organizational problems. The main difference between action research
and planned change is that action research places more emphasis on
diagnosing organizational problems and developing specific actions
to deal with specific problems, while planned change (although still
data-based) usually emphasizes preplanned organizational development techniques. Moreover, action research places greater emphasis on evaluation as a basis for further diagnosis and action planning than do planned change programs.

The cyclical nature of the action research model is illustrated in
French's framework presented in Figure 2–1. Overall, the following
seven basic stages are involved.[37]

1. *Problem identification.*   In this initial stage an individual in
   the organization, usually an upper-level executive, perceives
   that the organization has certain problems that might be
   ameliorated with the assistance of a behavioral science consultant (change agent).
2. *Consultation.*   The next phase usually entails joint discussion and collaboration of the perceived problems with a consultant. During this contact the two parties generally assist
   each other and assess the degree of "fit" between the organization's needs and the consultant's expertise.
3. *Data gathering and preliminary diagnosis.*   This phase is
   typically accomplished by the consultant, although in many
   organizations the consultant is assisted by a knowledgeable
   member of the organization. Especially if an external expert is
   employed, this assistance facilitates the consultant's entry into
   the organization. By utilizing the various forms of data-
   gathering techniques discussed earlier, the consultant generates initial data, engages in preliminary diagnosis, and tenta-
   tively analyzes the situation.
4. *Feedback to management.*   The analysis that results from the
   preliminary diagnosis of the data is then submitted to the top
   management group. Since action research is a collaborative
   process, these feedback and information-sharing sessions are
   quite valuable.
5. *Joint diagnosis and action planning.*   Once the initial data

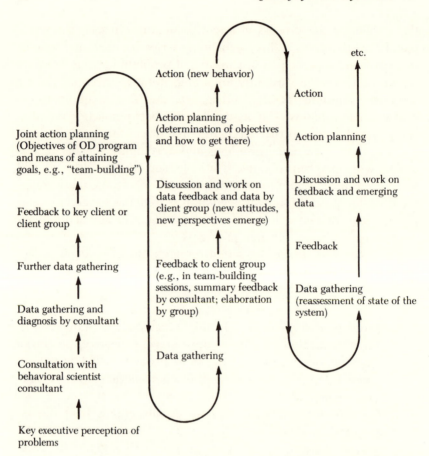

Figure 2-1 French's Action Research Model for Organization Development. (*Source: Wendell French, "Organization Development Objectives, Assumptions, and Strategies,"* California Management Review 12:2, 1969, p. 26. *Reprinted with permission of the* California Management Review.)

have been fed back to the executives involved, the consultant and management team discuss the meaning of the data, their implications, and needs for further diagnosis. A main theme of the action research model is that the consultant does not impose his or her own solutions; rather, from this joint deliberation the team develops possible courses of action to attain desired goals.

6. *Action.* During this phase of the process, the management team and the consultant agree on which actions should be taken. At this point, the action could be further data gather-

ing and a more in-depth look at specific aspects of a given situation. Obviously, this course depends considerably on the nature of the problem involved and could entail some repetition of steps 3 through 5 before any specific proposals are initiated.

7. *Evaluation.* Since action research is a cyclical process, data must also be gathered after any actions have been taken to monitor and assess the impact of the program. Based on this evaluation process, information is fed back to the management group, which in turn evokes further diagnosis of the situation, reanalysis of the problem, and new actions (solutions).

Intervention Theory, Planned Change, and Action Research: An Integration of Thoughts

Intervention theory, planned change, and action research overlap in that all three models emphasize (1) the use of behavioral science knowledge to improve organizational outcomes and (2) the involvement of organizational members and groups in the process. Moreover, all three models are aimed at producing effective and lasting (if desired) change in the organization.[38] Finally, all three approaches involve an interaction between a consultant and individuals within an organization, which results in an intervention that, in and of itself, may cause changes in that particular orientation.[39] However, each of these change techniques varies the emphasis on developing the problem-solving skills of the client organization's management. Both intervention theory and planned change, for example, place more of a stress on such learning than does action research. Furthermore, varying strengths and weaknesses characterize each approach.

Critics of intervention theory point out that it does not offer any research-based evidence that can support its underlying assumptions about the nature of organizations.[40] Moreover, since not all organizations are able to effectively make "free and informed" choices,[41] the approach's commitment to free choice may not be fully feasible.

Contrasted to the lack of research underlying intervention theory, planned change is grounded heavily in both theory and research. Unfortunately, little emphasis has been placed on measurement is-

sues and evaluation testing.[42] The main criticisms of the planned
change approach, however, do not focus fully on the model per se,
but rather on its application.[43] Basic problems stem from faulty diagnoses and the predetermination of many practitioners to employ
"favorite" techniques (for example, management by objectives, team
building and consultation, job enrichment, and so forth), as opposed
to seeking out the most appropriate technique that "fits" the situation confronting the organization.

While the action research model more fully emphasizes continued
diagnosis and evaluation of organizational problems and "solutions,"
it is often a costly and time-consuming process. In addition, since
one of the main aspects of action research is to develop new behavioral science knowledge to deal with organizational issues, in many
instances planned change is preferred because it focuses on the
application of previous knowledge.[44] Thus, planned change programs can provide a useful intervention mechanism where action
research may not be a viable alternative (due to cost, time, and so
forth). However, the essentially prepackaged nature of these efforts
can lead to a less effective strategy for a particular firm since these
programs are basically aimed at a more general audience.

The Cyclical Planned Intervention Model

Just as the different methods of collecting data can provide managers
with various perspectives on the nature of life in their organizations,
the three approaches to organizational change can also provide the
basis for devising strategies for improving the quality of employee
work life. The most appropriate data-gathering technique depends
on the type of information desired, the nature of the situation confronting the organization, the type and degree of management expertise, the level of trust in the groups involved, and so forth. Similarly, the rationales underlying intervention theory, planned
change, and action research can all contribute to the formalization of
a comprehensive survey feedback program. Thus, all of these approaches can be useful in developing an in-depth understanding
about a specific organization. The model that we employ in this book
is based on an integration of these different information-gathering
approaches and models of organizational change.

The process, which is referred to as the *Cyclical Planned Intervention Model*, is presented in Figure 2–2. This program entails the

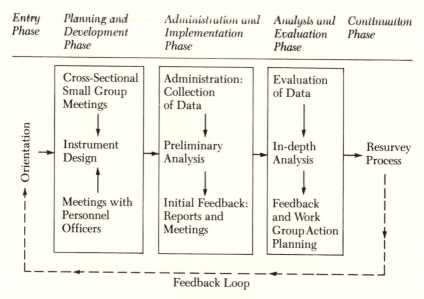

Entry Phase	Planning and Development Phase	Administration and Implementation Phase	Analysis and Evaluation Phase	Continuation Phase

Figure 2-2 Cyclical Planned Intervention Model.

following five-step process that forms the basis for the remainder of this book:

- Entry into the client organization
- Planning, diagnosis, and development of the survey-based program
- Implementation and administration
- Analysis, evaluation, and feedback
- Program continuation and organizational development

The framework is based on a planned intervention into an organization to assist the firm in generating valid—that is, explicit and verifiable—information about the attitudes and opinions of its employee population. Although the basic orientation of the process is preplanned, an action research component is built in, in that the design and evaluation of the instrument and overall program is done through diagnosis in joint consultation with managers and executives from the organization involved. As indicated in Table 2–2, although the process is encompassed under the rubric of survey feedback, the entire program relies on a number of different data-gathering techniques to ensure a comprehensive and systematic picture of the nature and quality of organizational life.

Table 2–2   Data Collection Techniques and Suggested Uses

Phase	Technique	Suggested Use
Entry	Interviewing; Polling	Discussions with managers/executives to find out organizational concerns, expertise of consultant, perceived problems, etc.
	Unobtrusive measures	Formal organization chart, recent copies of the house organ, etc. to get a fuller sense of organizational culture. Bulletin boards, office layout, and so forth are also useful.
Diagnosis/ Development	Interviewing	Selected key informants, especially managers who may have insights into organizational problems.
	Organization sensing	Small group meetings with cross section of employees to arrive at a fuller understanding of perceived problems, differences in orientations, etc.
	Polling	Meeting with personnel officers to feed back and discuss initial data.
	Observation	Observation of dynamics at sensing meetings, use of observations of managers, executives, employees in formulating survey questions.
Implementation	Survey questionnaire	Main data-gathering device to collect comprehensive and systematic attitudinal information from employee population.
	Polling	Feeding back initial information to different work groups for discussion and interpretation.
Evaluation	Polling	Feeding back information to different work groups for further discussion and interpretation of results.
	Unobtrusive measures	As part of analysis, useful to place organization in its proper social context.
Continuation	Unobtrusive measures	Impact of survey—for example, turnover, absenteeism statistics (longer-term).
	Polling	Reaction of work groups.
	Organization sensing	Use of follow-up groups to discuss results, impact of change, and implications for organization.

The Promise of Organizational Change

The survey-based feedback program suggested in the present volume is not a panacea to all organizational problems. Indeed, as will be discussed in Chapter 6, in some instances such a survey can raise employee expectations that, if not fulfilled, can lead to increased dissatisfaction. However, a comprehensive survey program, in which the results are fed back to the participants and then utilized to develop strategies for confronting organizational problems, can be a highly useful technique that should be considered in any decision making concerning the employee population. Since more and more employees today feel that they have a "right" to participate in any decisions having an impact on their jobs,[45] this process can alleviate many potential organizational problems. Moreover, it can facilitate the ongoing process of coping with change.

Traditionally, there have been two conceptual approaches to change in organizations: (1) reactive or adaptive change and (2) proactive change. The basic difference between these two orientations focuses on how change is handled. In the reactive mode a change occurs first, from either outside or inside the organization. Since organizations are open systems and are affected by these changes, the firm must adapt or adjust to its new environmental or situational context. Proactive change, by contrast, assumes that efforts to change emanate from within the organization as the organization anticipates *potential* needs or attempts to manipulate or control its environment toward a more favorable state. Thus, the organization initiates changes as it attempts to create a more desirable "fit" with its environment. Mintzberg's analysis of the nature of managerial work, for example, reflects these two orientations in terms of different types of decisions that managers are typically confronted with: the role of disturbance handler (reactive) and entrepreneur (proactive).[46]

From the managerial vantage point, these different conceptualizations of the change process can be transformed into types of strategies for managing change. In overseeing organizational adaptation to changing environmental conditions, managers can therefore approach change in a reactive, unplanned manner or in a proactive, anticipative manner. Of course, while not all of the contingencies involved can be predicted fully, by developing an awareness of the need for change managers can begin to anticipate potential problem areas and intervene before they actually become serious.

Reactive management, thus, is characterized by waiting until problems that can no longer be ignored emerge. This short-term, crisis-oriented management style often results in hasty decisions and an ineffective use of an organization's resources. *Anticipative management,* by contrast, refers to initiating organizational changes to deal with emerging conditions *before* they actually become problematic.[47] Perhaps an example can best illustrate the difference between these two approaches. Historically, American business has been slow to adjust to changing environmental conditions. Company policies and decision-making procedures, in many instances, have not kept pace with such changing public standards as employee health and safety, environmental protection, discrimination, and sexual harassment. During this period, the ways in which many employees reacted to these issues changed as well. Thus the orientations of the employee population and the organization itself were beginning to become increasingly strained. One of the recent repercussions of this strain has been "whistle blowing," a process where an employee goes beyond the management of his or her organization and "goes public" with the problem. The most visible examples of whistle blowing have been with Ford Motor Company's Pinto, Eastern Airlines' erratic autopilot mechanism, and the Michigan Chemical Company's poisonous fire retardant grain feed mixup.[48]

In most whistle blowing situations, however, the employees involved initially brought their problems to the organization's management. Unfortunately, many of these executives simply did not listen to the complaints but instead pushed them aside. Thus, rather than organizations' policing their own policies and dealing with these potential problems in an anticipative, proactive manner, we see many organizations reacting to charges against them. Recently, several organizations have been confronted by such accusations (charges of sexual harassment at General Electric and Yale University are two examples) and at the same time by such new legislation as Michigan's "Whistle Blower Protection Act," which encourages employees to sidestep any internal procedures for such complaints before releasing the information to the press and the public. Most likely, organizations would do better to try and anticipate problems and change the situation than to tersely cover them up.

Today's well-managed company must monitor such changes and evaluate how its employees are reacting to emerging environmental and job-related conditions. The ability to anticipate potential problems and to confront them in a proactive manner will be key elements of organizational effectiveness and efficiency. Of course, the great majority of issues affecting managers are not as controversial as the above examples, and every possible consequence that could emerge cannot always be predicted. However, organizational investment in its human resource capabilities can produce improved working relationships between the work force and the organization. Improving the quality of working life in the short term can have a longer-term impact on organizational efficiency, effectiveness, and productivity.[49]

Of course, considering the turbulent environment that confronts much of business today, many organizations believe the enhancement of employee concerns is of secondary importance. Grover Starling, for example, argues that:[50]

> *It is far from clear that a company grappling with high energy bills and burdensome federal regulations, when faced with fierce competition from foreign corporations or with capture by another company, will feel that its chances of survival will be enhanced because workers are represented in the decision-making process. As Sennett observes, it is ironic that our society should just now be struggling with the question of the quality of the experience of work. . . . Is discontent about working the ultimate luxury of late capitalism? Many employers believe the money, time, and effort put into responding to this discontent are a diversion of resources when the main task is surviving in an increasingly tough international economy. The simple answers to these problems would be an authoritarian, back-to-Theory X response. But, as H.L. Mencken said, to every knotty problem there is a solution — neat, simple, and wrong.*

A well-planned, comprehensive survey feedback program may not provide an organization with neat and simple answers to all its employee-related problems. It can, however, demonstrate to managers the areas requiring their attention in order to formulate more effective psychological contracts with their employees—in the short term, to improve the quality of work life, and in the longer term, to utilize more effectively the organization's human resources.

Endnotes

1. D. Yankelovich, *New Rules: Searching for Self-Fulfillment in a World Turned Upside Down* (New York: Random House, 1981).

2. W. Ouchi, *Theory Z: How American Business Can Meet the Japanese Challenge* (Reading, Mass.: Addison-Wesley, 1981).
3. R.T. Pascale and A.G. Athos, *The Art of Japanese Management: Applications for American Executives* (New York: Simon & Schuster, 1981).
4. N. Hatvany and V. Pucik, "An Integrated Management System: Lessons from the Japanese Experience," *Academy of Management Review* 6:3 (1981), pp. 469–80.
5. D. Hutchins, "Quality Circles—The Missing Link," *Leadership and Organization Development Journal* 1:4 (1980), pp. v–viii.
6. Hatvany and Pucik *op. cit.*; N. Hatvany and V. Pucik, "Japanese Management Practice and Productivity," *Organizational Dynamics* 9 (Spring 1981), pp. 4–21; H. Hazama, "Characteristics of Japanese-Style Management," *Japanese Economic Studies* 6:3–4 (1979), pp. 110–73; W. Ouchi and A.M. Jaeger, "Type Z Organization: Stability in the Midst of Mobility," *Academy of Management Review* 3:2 (1978), pp. 305–14.
7. R.E. Cole, *Work, Mobility, and Participation* (Berkeley: University of California Press, 1979).
8. R.E. Walton, "Quality of Work Life: What Is It?" *Sloan Management Review* 14:2 (1973), pp. 11–21; E. Huse, *Organization Development and Change* (New York: West, 1980); A. Nurick, "Some Issues in the Quality of Work Life," *Survey of Business*, University of Tennessee 12:3 (1977), pp. 18–22; A. Nurick, "Participation in Organizational Change: A Longitudinal Field Study," *Human Relations* (in press); J. O'Toole, *Work in America: Report of a Special Task Force to the Secretary of Health, Education and Welfare* (Cambridge, Mass.: MIT Press, 1973).
9. W. French and C. Bell, *Organizational Development* (Englewood Cliffs, N.J.: Prentice-Hall, 1978); D. Nadler, *Feedback and Organization Development* (Reading, Mass.: Addison-Wesley, 1977); D. Bowers, "O.D. Techniques and Their Results in 23 Organizations," *Journal of Applied Behavioral Science* 9:1 (1973), pp. 21–43; R. Golembiewski and R. Hilles, *Toward the Responsive Organization: The Theory and Practice of Survey Feedback* (Salt Lake City: Brighton Publishing, 1979); N. Margulies and A. Raia, *Conceptual Foundations of Organizational Development* (New York: McGraw-Hill, 1978); D. Bowers and J. Franklin, *Survey-Guided Development I: Data-Based Organizational Change* (La Jolla, Cal.: University Associates, 1977); D. Umstot, "Organization Development Technology and the Military: A Surprising Merger?" *Academy of Management Review* 5:2 (1980), pp. 189–202.
10. R.B. Dunham and F.J. Smith, *Organizational Surveys: An Internal Assessment of Organizational Health* (Glenview, Ill.: Scott, Foresman, 1979); N. Margulies and J. Wallace, *Organizational Change: Techniques and Applications* (Glenview, Ill.: Scott, Foresman, 1973); French and Bell, *op. cit.*
11. J. Annett, *Feedback and Human Behavior* (Baltimore: Penguin Books, 1969).
12. Dunham and Smith, *op. cit.*
13. D. Nadler and M. Tushman, "A Diagnostic Model for Organizational Behavior," in J.R. Hackman (ed.), *Perspectives on Behavior in Organizations* (New York: McGraw-Hill, 1977); D. Nadler and M. Tushman, "A Model for Diagnosing Organizational Behavior," *Organizational Dynamics* 9:2 (1980), pp. 35–51.

14. D. Nadler, *op. cit.;* W.G. Bennis, D.E. Berlew, E.H. Schein, and F.I. Steele, *Interpersonal Dynamics: Essays and Readings on Human Interaction* (Homewood, Ill.: Dorsey Press, 1973).

15. Hutchins, *op. cit.;* P.F. Drucker, "Learning from Foreign Management," *Wall Street Journal* (June 4, 1980), p. 24; U.C. Lehner, "Japanese Firms' Stress on Quality Control Is Reflected in Dogged Vying for Award," *Wall Street Journal* (September 24, 1980), p. 52.

16. Dunham and Smith, *op. cit.*

17. Margulies and Wallace, *op. cit.*

18. Huse, *op. cit.;* Nadler, *op. cit.;* J. Kotter, *Organizational Dynamics: Diagnosis and Intervention* (Reading, Mass.: Addison-Wesley, 1978); E. Webb, D. Campbell, R. Schwartz, and L. Sechrest, *Unobtrusive Measures: Nonreactive Research in the Social Sciences* (Chicago: Rand McNally, 1966); C. Selltiz, L. Wrightsman, and S. Cook, *Research Methods in the Social Sciences* (New York: Holt, Rinehart & Winston, 1976).

19. F.J. Smith, "The Index of Organizational Reactions," *JSAS Catalog of Selected Documents in Psychology 6*: ms. no. 1265 (1976); P.C. Smith, L.M. Kendall, and C.L. Hulin, *The Measurement of Satisfaction in Work and Retirement* (Chicago: Rand McNally, 1969); D.J. Weiss, R.V. Dawis, G.W. England, and L.H. Lofquist, *Manual for the Minnesota Satisfaction Questionnaire*, Minnesota Studies for Vocational Rehabilitation: XXII (University of Minnesota Industrial Relations Center, 1969).

20. C. Alderfer and L.D. Brown, "Questionnaire Design in Organizational Research," *Journal of Applied Psychology 56*:6 (1972), pp. 456–60.

21. R.L. Gold, "Roles in Sociological Field Observation," in N.K. Denizen (ed.), *Sociological Methods: A Sourcebook* (Chicago: Aldine-Atherton, 1970), pp. 370–80.

22. F. Roethlisberger and W. Dickson, *Management and the Worker* (Cambridge, Mass.: Harvard University Press, 1939); G. Homans, *The Human Group* (New York: Harcourt, Brace, 1950); E. Schein, *Organizational Psychology* (Englewood Cliffs, N.J.: Prentice-Hall, 1980); R.H. Franke and J.D. Kaul, "The Hawthorne Experiments: First Statistical Interpretation," *American Sociological Review 43*:5 (1978), pp. 623–43; B. Rice, "The Hawthorne Defect: Persistence of a Flawed Theory," *Psychology Today 16*:2 (1982), pp. 71–74.

23. E.J. Webb, *et al.*, *op. cit.*

24. Huse, *op. cit.*

25. C. Argyris, *Intervention Theory and Method* (Reading, Mass.: Addison-Wesley, 1970).

26. French and Bell, *op. cit.*, p. 102.

27. Huse, *op. cit.*, pp. 85–86.

28. R. Lippit, F. Watson, and B. Westley, *The Dynamics of Planned Change* (New York: Harcourt, Brace & World, 1958); M. Frohman and M. Sashkin, "The Practice of Organization Development: A Selective Review," Institute for Social Research, Technical Report (Ann Arbor: University of Michigan, 1970); D. Kolb and A. Frohman, "An Organization Development Approach to Consulting," *Sloan Management Review 12*:1 (1970), pp. 51–65.

29. Huse, *op. cit.;* E. Huse and J. Bowditch, *Behavior in Organizations: A Systems Approach to Managing* (Reading, Mass.: Addison-Wesley, 1977).

30. D. Harvey and D. Brown, *An Experiential Approach to Organization Development* (Englewood Cliffs, N.J.: Prentice-Hall, 1976).

31. R. Chin and K. Benne, "General Strategies for Effecting Changes in Human Systems," in W. Bennis, K. Benne, and R. Chin (eds.), *The Planning of Change* (New York: Holt, Rinehart & Winston, 1969), pp. 32–59.

32. A. Cohen, S. Fink, A. Gaddon, and R. Willits, *Effective Behavior in Organization* (Homewood, Ill.: Irwin, 1980).

33. J. French and B. Raven, "The Basis of Social Power," in D. Cartwright and A. Zander (eds.), *Group Dynamics: Research and Theory* (New York: Harper & Row, 1967).

34. D. J. Hickson, C.R. Hinings, C.A. Lee, R.E. Schneck, and J.M. Pennings, "A Strategic Contingencies' Theory of Intraorganizational Power," *Administrative Science Quarterly* 16:2 (June 1971), pp. 216–27.

35. Harvey and Brown, *op. cit.*

36. French and Bell, *op. cit.*

37. W. French, "Organization Development Objectives, Assumptions, and Strategies," *California Management Review* 12:2 (1969), pp. 23–34; Huse and Bowditch, *op. cit.*

38. Huse, *op. cit.*; Huse and Bowditch, *op. cit.*

39. Huse and Bowditch, *op. cit.*

40. M. Sashkin, W. Morris, and L. Horst, "A Comparison of Social and Organizational Change Models: Information Flow and Data Use Processes," *Psychological Review* 80:6 (1973), pp. 510–26.

41. E. Van De Vlunt, "Inconsistencies in the Argyris Intervention Theory," *Journal of Applied Behavioral Science* 13:4 (1977), pp. 557–64.

42. Sashkin, *et al.*, *op. cit.*

43. Huse, *op. cit.*

44. Huse, *op. cit.*; Huse and Bowditch, *op. cit.*

45. Yankelovich, *op. cit.*; M. Cooper, B. Morgan, P. Mortenson Foley, and L. Kaplan, "Changing Employee Values: Deepening Discontent?" *Harvard Business Review* 57:1 (1979), pp. 117–25.

46. H. Mintzberg, *The Nature of Managerial Work* (Englewood Cliffs, N.J.: Prentice-Hall, 1980).

47. Harvey and Brown, *op. cit.*

48. A. Westin, *Whistle Blowing* (New York: McGraw-Hill, 1980); A. Westin, "Michigan's Law to Protect the Whistle Blowers," *Wall Street Journal* (April 13, 1981), p. 26; A. Westin, "Employee Free Speech," *Wall Street Journal* (November 10, 1980), p. 25.

49. E. Mollander, *Responsive Capitalism* (New York: McGraw-Hill, 1980); G. Starling, *The Changing Environment of Business: A Managerial Approach* (Boston: Kent, 1980).

50. Starling, *op. cit.*, p. 488.

Chapter 3

PLANNING AND DEVELOPMENT
OF THE SURVEY

The planning and development of a quality of work life survey are clearly the most important phases of any comprehensive survey feedback program. Indeed, if these steps are done thoroughly and thoughtfully, any problems at latter stages are readily correctable. If, on the other hand, the planning and development are inadequate in any way, no analytic technique or data manipulation can overcome the resultant deficiencies. For this reason alone, allotting sufficient time to this initial stage is extremely important.

Time constraints, of course, are often the reason for taking shortcuts during the development of the survey instrument or for eliminating certain steps considered unnecessary. This was the case in one of our early surveys. Under considerable pressure to complete the process in a relatively short time period, the organization and consultants decided against pilot testing the instrument—a process by which the survey is given to a small sample of employees to assess and rectify ambiguous questions, readability problems, and response clarity. After all, it was reasoned, six people had screened the survey—including the consultants, the vice president of personnel, and the president—and everyone thought that it was clear and to the point. Unfortunately, a number of these "clear" questions were misunderstood by some of the organization's members. Consequently, these items had to be dropped from the analysis. Thus, while some time was saved in the development phase of the process, the end result was unusable data for certain questions.

In another instance, one of the authors helped analyze a survey in which the originators of the project had run into difficulty. Focusing on the effectiveness of campus ministries around the country, one of the survey questions asked, "How many fully ordained priests are working in your campus ministry program part-time?" A simple pilot test would have identified the absurdity that there is no such thing as a *partly* ordained priest.

Thus, the major concerns during the planning and development phase are to allow sufficient time for the process and to build in a series of checks and balances to minimize potential problems. If this is done, any problems that are inadvertently built into the procedure can be corrected. After a survey has been printed, it is too late to alter questions. Even though questions can be deleted from the analysis, including items that are of poor quality causes needless embarrassment. Moreover, since some people react negatively to surveys, such inclusions can reduce a survey's effectiveness by making it less than professional.

This chapter focuses on these initial activities, including the use of consultants, entry and preliminary diagnosis, and the actual process of survey development and question formulation. Within this context, we will also discuss the involvement of in-house personnel through sensing groups, sampling versus canvassing the population, and pilot testing.

The Use of Consultants: Internal Versus External

Attitude surveys may be conducted by either in-house professionals or external consultants. Much of the preparatory work, administrative activities, and distributional analyses are fairly straightforward and rather easily managed. Yet, although no set guidelines exist and such a survey can be conducted using internal personnel alone, doing so is unwise from several standpoints.

First, and perhaps the most important area of concern, is the issue of confidentiality. Because confidentiality is one of the most significant guarantees for obtaining accurate information, any doubts respondents have about where the information will go and who will be identified can subsequently bias the data. In many situations an organization's members may not fully trust the discretion of an organizational self-survey. If personnel do not feel that their responses and their anonymity will be safeguarded during the survey process, they may choose not to be completely truthful about some questions, or they may even omit some items altogether. In all attitude surveys we have conducted, confidentiality was one of the main points of concern raised by participants.

A second concern is that those working on the survey have experience in survey research, even if the research is in a different setting. Although much of the preparatory and administrative procedures are rather straightforward, a number of complex issues must be fully considered to ensure a sound and comprehensive program. Unless an individual has been trained in survey research procedures, many of the more subtle, intricate pitfalls may be missed.

With the exception of larger organizations that continually run such programs, most institutions and medium-sized companies employ outside consultants. Of course, cost and familiarity considerations can influence this decision. Unless the program is administered frequently, the cost of hiring an in-house professional would probably not be fully justified.[1] On the other hand, internal personnel usually have more knowledge of the organization and its workings than an external consultant. Thus, they may be able to add more insight into the reasons underlying certain trends in the data. One of the ways to resolve this problem is to have outside consultants work closely with in-house members who are knowledgeable about the organization. The close involvement of these individuals can further ensure continuity in the survey feedback process during the implementation of follow-up groups, which is a critical component of a successful development program.

If an organization decides to employ an external consultant, a number of issues should be considered in making the selection. Basically, a company can draw for consulting assistance from three main sources: local universities, private consultants, and management consulting firms. Depending on the needs of the organization and what it expects to achieve from the survey, each of these has its own advantages and disadvantages.

The main advantage of hiring consultants from local universities and colleges is that professors are likely to be knowledgeable about current research findings and methodological issues. This information can be quite valuable in developing the survey program and in analyzing the data. Moreover, professors are also likely to have access to their own institutional resources, such as computer facilities, library sources, and research assistance, at lower rates than consulting firms. Thus the cost of the consultation is apt to be less. Finally, university-based consultants usually conduct only one or two surveys during a given period and will generally have more flexibility in working with the client organization than a private consultant might have. The survey itself can be tailored to the organization's specific needs rather than simply using a canned program. The main disadvantage of using university-based consultants is that these individuals usually do not have access to industrywide norms or other sources of data for comparative analysis with similar institutions.

Private consultants and management consulting firms constitute the alternative resource base. The main advantage of this group, especially for the larger firms, is that they are likely to have conducted other surveys in similar types of institutions. Thus, they may have a data bank which will allow them to compare the client organization's quality of work life profile with similar organizational norms. In a relatively placid environment where feelings about work and work-related activities have remained fairly stable, such a data bank can provide the organization with base line information to assess its comparative posture. This base line profile of the industry can be useful in formulating policies and programs to deal with internal organizational problems. In a turbulent environment, however, the results from data collected even as recently as six months earlier may make the profile of the client institution appear to be more negative (or positive) than it would if the data were collected during the same period. Indeed, changes in the external environment of a firm, social and economic trends, political transitions, resource shortages, and people's sense of well being, among other societal factors, can affect the internal workings of an organization and the perceptions of its members. Thus, comparative data gathered one or two years earlier in a host of other organizations may be quite misleading to the client.

In order to develop this comparative base, consulting firms also tend to use canned programs instead of specific survey instruments developed to meet the individual needs of a particular institution. The items used will necessarily be general rather than personalized. While certain issues are, of course, important regardless of organizational type, many of the questions will not be critical for a particular firm. On the other hand, such survey packages have usually been tested for question reliability (that is, do survey items consistently tap attitudes and opinions?) and sometimes for validity (that is, do items measure what they purport to measure?).[2]

Thus, a major decision point early in the development process concerns the type of analysis the organization wants to undertake. Since attitudinal data are, by definition, relative, they should be assessed in comparison to some standard rather than in absolute terms. A one-time survey, of course, can provide an organization's management with descriptive data that can help the firm understand particular issues or problems. As such, this type of cross-sectional investigation can be beneficial. Yet, overall, whether part of an ongoing survey-based program or as a comparison to similar organizations in the industry or in a given geographical area, the resulting norms provide the context in which to assess the data. This interpretive process will be discussed in Chapter 5. The important point to be made here is that the decision about the kind of analysis to undertake must be made during this initial planning and development stage.

Either industry norms or past institutional findings can provide a useful basis for what an organization hopes to achieve. Useful data can often be collected by combining standardized questions with a series of tailor-made items focused on particular organizational concerns. Our own sense is that, in general, a tailor-made survey can provide a management team with more opportunity to listen to what the employees are saying, although at the cost of not being able to compare the organization against industry norms. As noted above, this problem is minimized in a turbulent environment in which industry norms are not meaningful.

In summary, the choice of consultants is usually based on availability, expertise, and degree of fit between what the individual consultant can offer and what the organization desires. Examples of the types of questions that should be asked in forming a client-consultant relationship for attitude survey work are summarized in Table 3–1.[3] Regardless of the type of consultant selected, however, internal organizational members should work closely with the consulting team to ensure continuity and the most effective use of feedback results.

Entering the Organization

Several points should be considered when hiring external consultants. Unless they have a long-term relationship with the organization, they will not know the issues that may have led to their hiring. Thus the consultants should first be briefed on the specific issues that are of concern. They should be given public information such as

Table 3–1   Parameters of the Client-Consultant Relationship: Survey-Based Organizational Development

---

GOALS
1. What are the goals of the relationship?
2. Are the roles of both the client and consultant understood and agreed upon?

DATA COLLECTION AND UTILIZATION
1. What kinds of data will be collected and how will they be gathered?
2. Who is responsible for survey administration? How will the survey be administered?
3. How many employees will be surveyed? How will they be selected?
4. Who will have access to the data? What form will this access take?
5. How will the data be used? What types of reports are to be generated (written, oral)? What statistics will be reported? What norms will the organization be compared with?
6. How will feedback be handled? How will results be communicated to employees?

LOGISTICS
1. What are the estimated time periods for the various activities?
2. What resources will be provided by the client? What resources will be provided by the consultant?
3. How will the project be evaluated?
4. What process will be used to review the relationship?

SOURCE: Based on David Nadler, *Feedback and Organization Development: Using Data-Based Methods* (Reading, Mass.: Addison-Wesley, 1977), pp. 89–94; Ron Zemke, "How to Pick an Employee Survey That Works—and Fits Your Needs," *Training: The Magazine of Human Resources Development* (June 1979), pp. 26–27.

organizational charts, the annual report, copies of the house organ, and any other information sources or policy statements that could help them understand the organization more fully.

To further facilitate entry into the organization, the consultants should also meet with a cross section of employees, including members of top management. Although not conclusive, most research suggests that outside intervention is more effective if the chief executive officer is behind the effort.[4] Such cooperation, of course, should involve more than a simple decision to allow a survey to take place. Indeed, management support should reflect a commitment to the program—in both its administration and its response to the data. The president, for example, should clearly state what the consultants were hired for, and assure organizational members of confidentiality by pointing out that the external consultants will be the only ones handling the raw data. As mentioned earlier, the issues of confidentiality and security of the instrument are very important. If members of the work force have any sense that they will be identified prior to or during the process of collecting the survey data or during the analysis, they may choose not to answer truthfully.

Although pertinent issues can change throughout a survey period, there are two problems that an organization should avoid. First, management should not withhold information that could subsequently make the survey trivial, irrelevant, or in any way oriented toward noncentral issues. Initially, consultants may not know the central issues, and they will often accept organizational guidance in formulation of the questionnaire. If employees perceive that a survey is being used to mask important issues, then both the organization's and the consultants' reputations are in jeopardy. The second issue focuses on the threat of unionization. Consultants should not be hired to conduct a survey and then use the data to advise the organization on how to avoid a union. One often-stated axiom is that those organizations that become unionized deserve it. This, of course, is a dramatic oversimplification; unions are common in some industries and uncommon in others. However, if unionization has emerged as an important issue and the organization decides to do an attitude survey, that the two are related will probably be a reasonable assumption. An attitude survey done under conditions of incipient unionization or a National Labor Relations Board election will have low credibility. Since trust and honesty are two important components for a successful quality of work life survey, any effort taken under these conditions may actually have an adverse impact.

Preliminary Diagnosis

Before designing the specific components of a survey feedback program, an initial analysis of the organization and its work-related activities is necessary. As delineated in Chapter 1, the fit between the organization's goals, structure, employee population, and decision-making systems should be assessed—a critical part of the entry process when consultants are employed. Discussions with key organizational personnel, continued familiarization with the organization, and interaction with the employee population will facilitate the development of an accurate survey instrument, establish an initial base for credibility, and set the foundation for a comprehensive program.

Discussions with Key Employees

Any preliminary diagnosis can be greatly facilitated by in-depth discussions and interviews with an organizational cross section of managers and employees. This information, combined with other written sources such as job descriptions, in-house newsletters, and training manuals, can lend important insight into the general climate and style of the organization. Without this sort of background work, many of the items included in the survey instrument may be only peripherally related or even meaningless to specific subgroups of employees because of their generality.

In one survey conducted by the authors in a banking institution, a tailor-made questionnaire was developed. Although this organization had conducted a survey nine years earlier, the issues and approach differed sufficiently to warrant the development of a new set of questions and a format that would lend itself to computer analysis. At the outset, the consultants, the personnel officer, and his assistant met together and discussed general issues that were thought to be appropriate for the survey. Early in the process, the consultants also met with the executive council, which consisted of a group of vice presidents and the chief executive officer, who generally set policy for the organization. This group provided helpful guidance and suggested key questions that were included in the survey. Thus, prior to developing questions or structuring the survey process, an in-depth discussion with senior bank personnel was undertaken to ensure an initial understanding of the bank's situation.

Formation of Sensing Groups

The next step employed in the bank survey was to assemble small groups of people throughout the company representing three different levels of the organization: workers, supervisors, and assistant vice presidents and other top managers. These groups were formed in an attempt to achieve a reasonable cross section of employees. As discussed in Chapter 2, this step should be accomplished for a number of reasons.

One basic reason this approach is employed is to make clear to organizational members that their assistance is an essential component in the survey process. Indeed, it is important for the organization as well as the consultants that the quality of work life survey be the subject of some positive, open discussion prior to its administration. Involving employees in this part of the development phase encourages a more complete sense of participation. People are usually prompted to begin talking about the survey, and the resulting publicity can heighten interest for the time when the survey itself is actually given.

Second, these groups can provide the consultants and management with a more complete overview of issues that are of primary importance to the employee population. Indeed, the pool of questions that form the core of the survey often emerges from these discussions. Even though some of the points raised in these meetings might not necessarily be incorporated into the survey instrument per se, they can lend insight into the analysis of the survey data and raise points that should be considered by the organization's management. Finally, meeting with the consultants can further emphasize the confidentiality of the process. The fact that individuals outside the organization are handling the raw data and are only supplying aggregate information to the company encourages more open participation and more truthful responses.

In the bank survey we have been using as an example, three different groups, which met at different times, were formed. Each group was composed of approximately twenty to twenty-five people and was representative of either the employee population, supervisors, or mid-level management. These groups were formed to encourage fuller participation since people tend to be less inhibited when they are among people with similar organizational status.

Each session, which lasted about two hours, was broken into three segments. Initially, participants were divided into four smaller groups of five or six. Although these groups were created on a cross-sectional basis, for practical reasons no persons with any reporting relationships were allowed within groups. Two general questions were used to initiate thought and discussion: (1) "If you were developing an attitude survey for the bank, what questions would you have the bank ask its employees?" (2) "What things would *you* really like to tell the bank?" Participants were instructed to jot down any items that came to mind before the discussion began so that the points that would subsequently be raised would not be overly influenced by one major theme. Once this initial note-taking was completed, a recorder from each group was chosen to keep notes on the group's discussion, which lasted for approximately forty-five minutes.

After reproducing and disseminating the notes so that each group had copies of the other group's discussion, the second segment of the session focused on sharing the information. Under the leadership of the consultants, the data were openly discussed. This process contributes to the anonymity of individual comments. For example, it is much easier for an individual to initiate conversation by taking a potentially controversial point from one of the sheets rather than by giving the impression that it is his or her own idea. Moreover, the overlapping of group discussions lends more anonymity to the process and corroborates important issues.

Finally, during the last segment of the small group sensing session, comments were summarized and reasons underlying certain points were clarified. The meeting ended with a debriefing and an explanation of how this information would be used to develop the survey questions, to clarify information in analyzing the data, and ultimately to write the final report. Thus, as the preceding discussion points out, involving in-house personnel is a critically important part of the development phase. If individuals at all levels of an organization are included, are guaranteed confidentiality and anonymity, and are encouraged that their input will have an impact on the survey, the outcome will readily improve the instrument itself, its implementation, and its analysis. Although this process may be somewhat time-consuming, the end result more than warrants the effort.

Development of the Survey

In moving from the preliminary diagnosis to the development of the survey itself, a number of issues must be considered. The first concerns the selection of target groups and specific categories of employees who should be analyzed separately. This selection process relates to the appropriate groups and related sociodemographic, job, and organizational data that should be included in the survey. The second point deals with the decision to canvass or sample the populations. This issue focuses predominantly on applicability of the instrument and organizational representation. Another area of concern relates to the different categories of questions and specific attitudinal facets that should be included. Finally, the types of questions and scaling techniques to be employed must also be considered.

Target Groups

One of the first decisions that must be made concerns the employee population to be surveyed. Which employees should be included in the survey? Should all job clusters and levels of the organization be involved? Should the survey focus only on full-time employees, or also include part-timers? Obviously, there are no set answers to any of these questions, and to a large extent the decision should be based on the reasons the organization is undertaking the survey.

Traditionally, attitude surveys have focused almost totally on nonmanagement personnel. In fact, attempts to measure the attitudes of managers and executives constitute a relatively recent phenomenon. These efforts, however, have shown the utility of such a broader focus. Indeed, since mid- and upper-level managers often have a more global understanding of companywide policies, programs, and problems, their input can be valuable in making decisions based on the survey data.[5]

Of course, while some issues will be pertinent to both employees and managers alike, certain areas will be of greater concern to higher-status employees. A subset of questions that is oriented toward this latter group can be included at the end of the overall organizational survey. Thus the same instrument can be used throughout the organization to provide a sound base for internal comparisons, and at the same time the perceptions of managers can be compared to those of the nonmanagement group.

Another group that must be considered is the part-time employee population. In many banking institutions, for example, the trend is toward using part-timers in a number of line positions, especially as tellers. These individuals may very well have quite different orientations to the job, related working conditions, and the organization than the full-time population. Thus, to assess fully the impact of the job on these individuals and the reverse, their inclusion in such a survey usually is warranted.

Because part-timers are likely to hold quite different attitudes than the full-time group, however, analyzing the two subsets separately is more effective. Usually, two separate reports should be prepared, although there might be a section in the overall report comparing and contrasting the two groups. This has been the general procedure we have followed in our own survey programs. Inclusion of the part-time group, of course, can contribute to additional scheduling problems and other administrative difficulties.

Sample Versus Entire Population

A related decision that the organization and the consultants must make is whether to canvass the entire population or to base the survey on a sample of employees. Since the ramifications to this decision are important, they are summarized briefly as follows:

Advantages of Population Survey	Advantages of Sample Survey
Greater institutional credibility	Lower cost
Simpler analytical techniques	Fewer materials to prepare
More easily interpretable data	Smaller magnitude

In general, a population survey is preferable to a sample survey. If the intention of an organizational survey is simply to gather information on employee feelings about a particular set of issues, then a sample design that would minimize costs and work loads would be appropriate. Clearly, if there are 10,000 persons in an organization that is to undergo a quality of work life survey assessment, surveying a sample of 500 respondents will be more practical and easier than canvassing the entire work force. Especially when open-ended questions that must be hand-coded prior to analysis are used, anything over 200 to 300 respondents can become a time-consuming and costly effort. To a lesser degree, the same is true for the closed-ended questions. Answer sheet and questionnaire printing also becomes more costly, preparation times increase, and the logistical problems of administration become more complex with large numbers.

At the same time, a population survey has higher credibility than a sample survey because it involves virtually everyone in the organization. Potential respondents who disagree with the findings of a sample survey often attribute the findings to an inadequate sample. Because most employees participate in a population survey, even if the findings are contrary to what a specific group might think, the credibility of the survey process will remain intact. Moreover, the survey-based approach used in this book places more stress on employee participation. By involving all employees in the survey process, the overall outcome of the project can be greatly enhanced.

If for time- and cost-related reasons a sample approach is chosen, one of the main issues that must be considered is the minimization of bias in the selection procedure. Since the purpose of sampling is to gather information about an entire population (in this case, the organizational work force) by surveying a proportion of that group, reliable procedures that will increase the probability of true representation must be employed.[6] In organizational surveys, selection bias can arise (1) if the sampling is accomplished on a nonrandom basis (that is, the selection is either consciously or unconsciously influenced by human choice), (2) if the sampling frame that serves as the basis for selection does not adequately cover the population, or (3) if certain sections of the population refuse to participate (nonresponse). Thus, probability sampling is the prime method that can be used to provide data from a given sample which accurately represent the responses that could be gathered from the entire population.

Random Sampling. The most commonly used form of probability sampling is referred to as *simple random sampling*, a process in which any member of the population has an equal chance of being selected. This is accomplished through sampling *without* replacement—that is, an individual cannot appear in the sample more than once. To ensure randomness, individuals are chosen either on the basis of a table of random numbers, which can be found in most elementary statistics texts, or by the "lottery method" (each member of the population is represented by a token—the tokens are placed in a bin and drawn until the required sample size is selected). Although random sampling is often equated with "haphazard selection" and although many people believe that as long as the investigator does not consciously select certain individuals randomness can be ensured, this is, in fact, not the case. Individuals unconsciously tend to favor certain people or units in the population even if they think they are choosing randomly. Only by undertaking a procedure that is independent of human judgment can the sample be said to be truly random.[7]

Stratified Sampling. An important variation on probability sampling that is often used in organizational settings is *stratified sampling*. The approach is to increase the precision of a particular sample by ensuring that certain critical groups are correctly represented. This method does not imply a departure from the principle of randomness. Rather, *prior to* selection, the population is divided into critical groups (sexes, races, job clusters, and so forth); the next step is a random sample selected *within* each group. Although this method can increase the precision of sample representativeness compared with simple random sampling, the choice within groups must be randomly made.[8]

Cluster Sampling. A second variation on probability sampling, which can further reduce survey costs, is *cluster sampling.* Although used less frequently than simple random sampling or stratified sampling, cluster sampling is a process of sampling complete groups or units within a given population. This is often done through a multi-stage process in which different work groups or teams are randomly selected and included in the sample. In an organization, however, there is often a question concerning what actually constitutes an appropriate cluster for analysis. Since this is a highly judgmental decision, the expertise of the survey administrator is especially important.[9]

A final consideration of employing a sampling survey as opposed to a population survey is related to the nature of data analysis. In a population survey, because there is no need to generalize from one group to a larger group, percentages or means to identify the distribution of responses across participants can be used. Virtually everyone knows how to interpret these data. In contrast, if a sample survey has been conducted in conjunction with the use of percentages or means, certain statistical tests must also be used to assure that the populations from which the samples were obtained are or are not significantly different.

Nonresponse

Nonresponse is a problem that confronts all survey researchers since the data collection process is never totally under their control. The problem of nonresponse applies to both organizational canvassing and sample surveys. With a well-designed survey program, however, the potential of bias arising from nonresponse can be minimized.[10]

The main issue is not that nonresponse can lead to a reduced sample, but rather that poor response rates are not usually part of a random process—that is, nonresponse to social or organizational surveys has its own determinants, which typically vary from survey to survey.[11] As a way of clarifying this problem, picture a survey population as being composed of two subpopulations—those who respond to the survey and those who do not.[12] Although this analogy is an oversimplification, the important point is that the researcher must determine the extent to which the two groups differ from one another. If, for instance, bank tellers obviously have a much lower participation rate in the survey than other job categories, then the conclusions that can be drawn relative to the teller group will be less conclusive than those drawn from the other job clusters. Moreover, the lack of certainty can then distort the general picture drawn about the organization.

This bias, of course, can be minimized in a number of ways. Since mail surveys tend to have higher nonresponse rates than surveys completed during work hours on the organization's premises, one way of reducing the number of people who do not fill out surveys is to administer the instrument during the workday. Another approach is to transmit in advance to the employee population the importance of the survey. Involving individuals in the process of formulating the questions, discussing issues with them, and promoting the survey can all reduce a lack of willingness to participate. These approaches will be discussed further in Chapter 4.

If the nonresponse rate is still relatively large, however, it is important to focus on that group and attempt to transform as many of these employees as possible into respondents. Then, by comparing the responses of the two groups (that is, those who initially participated versus those who initially refused), statistical tests can indicate if any significant differences exist. If the differences in response are not statistically significant, then it is safe to generalize from the data to the entire population with more confidence than if the differences were statistically significant. There are ways, however, to adjust statistically for any bias due to nonresponse with which professional surveyors are familiar.[13] The main point is that to ensure that the data are truly representative of the employee population, the potential bias arising from nonresponse to the survey must be minimized.

Sociodemographic Data

Although assessing the overall climate or atmosphere within an organization is important, being able to distinguish between responses for significant subgroups of the population is also useful. How do racial minorities view the organization's Equal Employment Opportunity program compared with majority group members? Do all facets of the organization perceive training needs in the same perspective? Does one job cluster experience different types of problems from other job groupings?

Such analyses can be readily accomplished through cross-tabulation, which will be discussed in Chapter 5. However, unless the survey includes appropriate background information, these questions will remain unresolved. Many organizations, for example, discover during analysis of their data that they do not have sufficient detail to address some issues fully. Thus, information of this type should be given ample consideration during the preliminary phase of the process. In many organizational surveys, sociodemographic data often include the following information: (1) where in the organization the individual works, (2) salary, (3) age, (4) length of time employed, (5) number of previous full-time jobs, (6) level of education, (7) job duties, (8) sex, (9) racial background, and (10) level of authority within the organization. These data allow the surveyor to classify or cross-tabulate the respondents by one or more of these variables to locate potential pockets of discontent, specific problems, or even unusually high satisfaction with the job.

Major Subsections of the Survey

Because the categories of questions form the core of the survey, this part of the development process is perhaps the most important phase. Ordinarily, such surveys focus on a range of organizational and job-related facets such as compensation, supervision, working conditions, commitment, and job satisfaction. Some surveys focus more explicitly on specific issues such as training needs, but these are often employed as a supplement to a broader overview of the organization. [14]

Comprehensive survey-based programs often include questions on the following quality of work life issues, many of which were discussed briefly in Chapter 2:

- Overall organization (feelings and commitment)
- Compensation issues (pay and benefits)
- Job security
- Management (policies)
- Immediate supervisor (relations with)
- Advancement issues
- Co-worker and interpersonal relations
- The job itself (characteristics, demand, satisfaction)

Of course, the various issues that are important to a particular organization should be clarified during the preliminary diagnosis, discussion, and sensing group stages. In a recent survey we conducted for a banking institution, for example, questions were added concerning employee reactions to the organization's stance and involvement in a number of public policy issues.

Question Design

During the actual formulation of the survey instrument, question design should consider the process of data management and analysis as well as how easily the respondent can understand the directions and format of the questionnaire. Design issues in the actual format of the questionnaire itself will be discussed in Chapter 4. This section focuses on the different types of questions that can be used in surveying employee attitudes about various aspects in the quality of work life. The discussion compares open- and closed-ended questions and delves into Likert-type attitudinal scales, question wording, response sets, and the importance of conducting a pilot test.

Open-Ended Versus Closed-Ended Questions. In general, all questions are either "open" or "closed." A closed-ended question is one in which the respondent is asked to choose between a series of structured replies. In open-ended questions respondents decide the nature, detail, and length of their answers in a spontaneous, unchecked manner. Examples of the two types of questions are shown below:

Closed-Ended "Likert" style:
  Overall, I am satisfied with my job.   Strongly agree   _____
                                        Agree   _____
                                          Uncertain   _____
                                          Disagree   _____
                                          Strongly disagree   _____

Open-Ended:
  The things I like most about my job are: _____
  _____
  _____
  _____
  The things I like least about my job are: _____
  _____
  _____
  _____

Obviously, there are advantages and disadvantages to both types of question. Although richer data and deeper insight into specific issues can be obtained through the use of open-ended questions, they are also time-consuming and difficult to analyze. While closed-ended questions can be quantified in a much more straightforward manner and are easier and quicker to answer, there is a loss of spontaneity and expressiveness on the part of the respondent.

Normally, open-ended questions are used more extensively in preliminary diagnosis than in the survey itself because of the time factor. During initial diagnosis, when the consultants and managers are trying to delineate the important issues for a particular organization, this type of "free" response is invaluable. In the early sensing sessions, open-ended questions are used to generate initial discussions and to seek out important issues. Once these areas are identified, however, they often can be transformed into closed-ended questions, which then can be given to a larger population more efficiently than open-ended questions.

Although most of the questions used in surveys are closed-ended, respondents should have an opportunity to tell the organization what is on their minds. Open-ended questions that ask the respondent to list the things they like best and the things they like least about the organization, for instance, may elicit data that would otherwise remain buried. Similarly, some questions may be more conveniently put in open-ended rather than closed-ended form.

In one of the bank surveys, effectiveness of the training programs emerged as a critical issue. Rather than a series of closed-ended questions that focused on different aspects of these programs, a general item was used to measure overall satisfaction/dissatisfaction with the training programs in question. This item was followed by an opportunity for the respondent dissatisfied with the programs to state specifically the unsatisfactory aspects. Thus the organization received a number of specific complaints and suggestions as to how the training program could be improved. These data were used subsequently by the new training manager to restructure certain aspects of training.

The formats for surveys differ, of course, usually depending on the number of respondents included. These differences will be discussed in Chapter 5, which concerns survey administration. A brief discussion about how open- and closed-ended questions can be integrated, however, is warranted. As with the example given above, if the survey population is small enough (for example, under 350 respondents), the following approach can be quite effective:

The performance evaluation system is fair.   Strongly agree   _____
(If you disagree, please state why.) _____   Agree   _____
_____   Neutral   _____
_____   Disagree   _____
_____   Strongly disagree   _____

The main advantage of this approach is that when the questionnaire is being tabulated for key punching and statistical analysis, the content of the open-ended responses may be coded and catalogued for inclusion in the statistical analysis. This coding procedure will be discussed in more detail in the data analysis section of Chapter 5. For surveys of larger populations, optical scanning forms are usually employed (see Chapter 4). In this instance instructions for comments about specific questions can be given on the questionnaire, and the open-ended responses can be placed on a separate sheet of paper. In very large surveys usually the open-ended questions will be sampled, the assumption being that once two hundred or so responses have been examined, very little new information will be found.

Question Format. In the closed-ended question examples given above, responses were cast in a modified Likert-type attitudinal scale. A number of other scaling techniques are sometimes employed in survey research, including Thurstone scales, Guttman scales, Osgood's Semantic Differential, and scales measuring social distance. These scales differ in the level of "measurement sophistication" required of the data (from nominal level to data that are ordinal or interval in nature).* However, since the reliability of Likert-type scales tends to be good,[15] they are used extensively in organizational research. Essentially, respondents are asked to place themselves on a continuum—ranging from "strongly agree" to "agree," "neutral or uncertain," "disagree," and finally to "strongly disagree"—in terms of their attitudes about a particular issue. Although five categories are normally used, in some instances three or seven categories have been employed. Complex scoring methods are often utilized, sometimes by transforming the data into a normal distribution, but research has indicated that these statistically sophisticated measures are little more effective than a simple ranking of 1, 2, 3, 4, and 5.[16]

In using Likert-type scales to measure attitudes, variation between positively and negatively stated items is suggested. This variation, to be discussed more fully under problems of response sets,

---

* A fuller discussion of these other scaling techniques is available in most research texts. Excellent discussions can be found in Claus Moser and G. Kalton's *Survey Methods in Social Investigation* (New York: Basic Books, 1974), Chapter 14; and A.N. Oppenheim's *Questionnaire Design and Attitude Measurement* (New York: Basic Books, 1966), Chapter 6.

forces respondents to be more careful in their response to each item, rather than automatically answering all questions in the same manner.

Occasionally, questions can be inserted with different continuums:

The benefits at (organization name) are:	Excellent	____
	Good	____
	Fair	____
	Poor	____

The flexitime system is ____ to me.	Very important	____
	Fairly important	____
	Not so important	____
	Not important at all	____

Again, these questions are often included to break up the monotony of large numbers of similar-sounding questions. They force respondents to think more clearly about their answers. Moreover, developing a response continuum that fits the question as well as possible is very important.

Frame of Reference Questions. Another concern in organizational surveys often focuses on the reasons why people feel the way they do about particular issues. If, for instance, the organization expects that there might be a relatively strong negative response regarding satisfaction with pay, a question asking respondents to name the group they are comparing themselves to in formulating their judgment can be useful. In one of our surveys for a research laboratory, many of the longer-term respondents still referred to the old organizational structure in existence when the laboratory was part of a major university. In early discussions with employees, we found that these individuals compared their position at the laboratory with their colleagues who were working for the university— even though they were now part of two separate institutions. In order to assess how extensive this identification with the old organizational structure was, a series of "frame of reference" questions were added for key issues. For example:

I am paid fairly for the work I do.	Strongly agree	____
	Agree	____
	Neutral	____
	Disagree	____
	Strongly disagree	____

The basis for my response to the preceding question is:

Pay at (the laboratory)	____
Pay compared to (the university)	____
Pay outside (the laboratory and the university)	____
My own sense of what my job is worth	____

Such data can give an organization a clearer indication of why people feel the way they do about a given issue. In turn, this can lend insight into effective ways of dealing with potential and present problem areas.

Question Wording

A review of the literature on the wording of questions in surveys concluded that the evidence is somewhat bewildering.[17] Many of the arguments are contradictory, and, unfortunately, constructing general principles from them is difficult. The one basic point of agreement is that the writing of questions is an art that requires skill as well as sensitivity to the audience involved.[18] Entire books have been written on the subject of how to formulate questions for survey research, and the reader is encouraged to consult these for further clarification.[19]

In writing questions for a particular survey, the individuals involved must consider the abilities and educational level of the population being surveyed, the purpose of the survey, and the placement of questions next to other questions in the questionnaire.[20] Thus, a list of "how to's" can only serve as general guidelines and cannot be considered as absolute principles. Rather than simply focusing on what should be done in writing questions, pointing out typical problems and pitfalls in question design is perhaps equally, if not more, beneficial.

Response Sets. A response set is a predisposition to answer a question in a particular way. This is especially applicable to attitudinal items in which respondents reply in a set manner, almost independent of context. A number of such response tendencies have been identified: *social desirability*, the tendency to agree with items the respondent believes to reflect socially (or organizationally) desirable attitudes;[21] *acquiescence*, the tendency to either agree or disagree with questions in general;[22] and *extremity*, the tendency either to use or to avoid using extremes.[23]

The acquiescence bias is one of the classic problems in questionnaire analysis. Individuals who respond in this manner are often referred to as "yea-sayers" and "nay-sayers." Some respondents by their nature will mark down that they "strongly agree" with everything, or "strongly disagree" with everything, regardless of the content of the question. The problem is that for these people outside influences may be determining their responses as opposed to conditions within the organization. If yea-saying or nay-saying appears to be a problem, a program that will cull out a given percentage of extreme respondents on both sides should be developed and the survey reanalyzed.

Another response problem related to the extremity bias is a central tendency response set in which the respondent excessively uses the middle "neutral, neither agree nor disagree" category. A large group of people using this category across all of the issues may mean that respondents fear that their identity will be compromised. A final kind of response set is the halo effect, a conceptual respondent bias. When one characteristic, often a noncentral issue, colors the perception of the respondent over a number of related issues, the respondent is operating under the halo effect response set. For instance, the male respondent who feels negatively about the role of women in industry may color the entire section of questions that deal with "relations with supervisors" if his supervisor is a woman. Similarly, if a respondent perceives one aspect of the organization in extremely favorable terms, this could positively influence his or her perception about other aspects of the institution and its members. Identifying a respondent working under the halo effect is easier in a performance appraisal than in an attitude survey; however, care should be taken in the development of survey items that personal biases are screened out as much as possible.

A related response problem is a general tendency to respond to blocks of questions in a similar way, regardless of the meaning of the item. For instance, if all questions in a block are phrased positively (that is, in a way that "strongly agree" is the most favorable response), a potential problem is that a respondent's previous answer, or group of answers, can determine the response to a subsequent question. Similarly, if a group of questions concerned with issues of pay is followed by a block of questions about benefits, and if there is general dissatisfaction with pay, the gloom about pay may influence the responses to benefits even if there is general satisfaction with them.

Thus, inserting questions that may be stated positively, but for which the most favorable answer is "strongly disagree," can be useful. One such statement might be "Sexual harassment is a frequent occurrence in the office." If this type of statement is inserted, along with a group of statements to which a positive response is favorable (for example, "My medical plan is equal to or better than the industry norm"), the respondent is forced to read each item carefully. Another approach to ensure that respondents read questionnaire items with care concerns the placement of questions within the survey. Although items are assigned to specific categories for analysis purposes (for example, compensation issues, immediate supervisor, working conditions, aspects of the job, and so forth), questions may either be grouped together or placed randomly in the questionnaire. Our preference is to disperse category items throughout the survey.

Leading Questions. Another concern in questionnaire development is preparing questions in a neutral way to prevent the appearance of a socially desirable response. For instance, if the researchers want to know about attitudes concerning the effectiveness of a recent organizational restructure, they are better off stating briefly that "The organizational restructure has improved communication between departments," than "The organizational restructure has improved the ineffective communication between departments."

At times, however, using questions that are both mildly positive and mildly negative is more effective in coming up with a complete picture. For instance, after stating, "Overall, I am satisfied with my pay," it may be appropriate to state "Pay in this organization has kept up with local salary trends" (a mildly leading question) and "Pay has kept up with inflation in the past two years." Thus the researcher has prepared a collage of questions that address many sides of the pay issue.

Double-Barreled Questions. Care must be exercised not to create questions that have multiple parts, one part of which may be perceived differently from another. "Overall, I am satisfied with my pay and benefits" is an innocuous-looking statement, but if the respondent is satisfied with benefits, but not the pay, there is going to be confusion as to how to answer the question. In these cases, separating the issues into two separate statements is best.

Misleading Questions. Questions that are clearly misleading or confusing are reasonably easy to pick out after a pilot test; sometimes, however, even a prescreening and pilot test will not identify a misleading question. One experience the authors had involved a statement posed to bank middle managers: "Top management is responsive to the needs of my people." This item went through the usual pilot testing with no difficulty. When the authors cross-tabulated the responses by race, however, it was apparent that minority middle managers interpreted the phrase "my people" to mean other minorities, while nonminority supervisors interpreted the same phrase to mean people who worked for them. Since this was a case of dual interpretation, the item had to be eliminated from the final analysis.

In an early attempt to examine the potential overuse of the middle response category—"neutral, neither agree nor disagree"—which can be used by persons who are *in fact* neutral as well as by people who do not understand a question or item, the authors also used an "I do not understand the question" category in the surveys. However, in a few items, the word "understand" was also used in the question, such as "I understand how the job posting system works." The problem was that some people who understood the meaning of the question perfectly well used the final category "I do not understand the question" to indicate that they did not realize how the process of job posting worked, rather than its intended use of alerting the researchers to the fact that they had included a confusing question.

As is evident, a whole host of item construction problems have to be avoided. In brief, the following are some principles of question-naire construction that may be helpful in writing questionnaire items.[24]

1. *Use simple language.*   The main aim in question wording is to communicate to respondents as nearly as possible in their own language. Technical terms and jargon that will not be understood by the population you are surveying should be avoided. However, you should also avoid the appearance of "talking down" to the respondents.

2. *Use short questions.*   Long questions can become very complex, eventually even leading to the "double-barreled question" problem. While an occasional long question may clarify a specific situation, these should be kept to a minimum since they reduce the survey-taking tolerance of respondents and increase the chance for misunderstanding.

3. *Be precise.*   Ambiguous and vague questions are particularly damaging to surveys. If a particular question is at all ambiguous, it is

likely to be interpreted in a number of different ways by different employees, and will be useless. Vague questions produce vague responses. In closed-ended questions the response choices are part of the question; thus these alternatives should be clearly focused. Still, in a desire to avoid vagueness in questions, many items become so precise that they are hard to answer or seem trivial. The following is an example of this pitfall:

Too Vague:

How often did you discuss job-related problems with your supervisor this past year?

Never	____
Rarely	____
Occasionally	____
Regularly	____

Too Precise:

How often did you discuss job-related problems with your supervisor this past year?

Number of times	____

Revision:

How often did you discuss job-related problems with your supervisor this past year?

Not at all	____
A few times	____
About once a month	____
About 2–3 times a month	____
About once a week	____
More than once a week	____

Pilot Testing

Before an attitude questionnaire is reproduced for general use, pilot testing must be done. Although one reference book suggests that a group be formed to "talk through" the questionnaire,[25] this step is really in addition to what might be done on a pilot study. Actually carrying out a miniature survey under the exact conditions in which it will be conducted later on and then talking it through with the group is more effective. By conducting a miniature survey, and then discussing it, the surveyors find out not only whether the items are clear, but also whether the instructions are clear, whether respondents believe that confidentiality exists, whether respondents know how to fill out the forms, and so forth. Pilot testing of about twelve to fifteen people is crucial to the success of an attitude survey because it allows the researchers to make any corrections to items and instructions that are not clear.

Summary

This chapter has made a strong case for careful planning in survey research. Planning and pilot testing are the only ways that researchers can know that everything is clear and that nothing important is omitted. This phase should not be rushed. Including as many persons in the development of a survey as is recommended may seem cumbersome, but the more points of view expressed, the less the chance that costly errors will be made.

In the process of developing the survey and instructions, the pilot test is the final check against faulty assumptions made by the researchers or managers. The pilot test can also serve as an additional check on how clear the instructions and the instruments are to persons who perhaps have different kinds of educational backgrounds and who might not be in a position to "read between the lines" as to what might be desired on the survey. In brief, delaying the administration of a survey because of questions about its construction is far preferable to administering a badly constructed survey. Although time may be saved by completing this initial phase quickly, the entire survey process can subsequently suffer.

Endnotes

1. R. Dunham and F. Smith, *Organizational Surveys: An Internal Assessment of Organizational Health* (Glenview, Ill.: Scott, Foresman, 1979); R. Zemke, "How to Pick an Employee Survey That Works—And Fits Your Needs," *Training: The Magazine of Human Resources Development* (June 1979), pp. 26–27.
2. Zemke, *Ibid.*; R. Zemke, "Resources for Surveying Employee Attitudes and Opinions," *Training: The Magazine of Human Resources Development* (June 1979), pp. 28–33.
3. D. Nadler, *Feedback and Organization Development: Using Data-Based Methods* (Reading, Mass.: Addison-Wesley, 1977); R. Zemke, "How to Pick an Employee Survey," *op. cit.*
4. M. Beer and E.F. Huse, "A Systems Approach to Organization Development," *The Journal of Applied Behavioral Science* 8:1 (1972), pp. 79–101.
5. Dunham and Smith, *op. cit.*

6. C. Moser and G. Kalton, *Survey Methods in Social Investigation* (New York: Basic Books, 1974), see Chapters 5–7.
7. *Ibid.*, pp. 80–85.
8. *Ibid.*, pp. 85–93.
9. *Ibid.*, pp. 100–107.
10. *Ibid.*, pp. 166–87.
11. A. Oppenheim, *Questionnaire Design and Attitude Measurement* (New York: Basic Books, 1966), see Chapter 2.
12. Moser and Kalton, *op. cit.*
13. *Ibid.*
14. Dunham and Smith, *op. cit.*
15. Oppenheim, *op. cit.*, see Chapter 6.
16. *Ibid.;* Moser and Kalton, *op. cit.*, Chapter 14.
17. Moser and Kalton, *op. cit.*, pp. 318–41.
18. Oppenheim, *op. cit.*, Chapter 3; Dunham and Smith, *op. cit.*, pp. 80–82.
19. S.L. Payne, *The Art of Asking Questions* (Princeton, N.J.: Princeton University Press, 1951); R.L. Kahn and C.F. Cannell, *The Dynamics of Interviewing* (New York: Wiley, 1957), Chapter 5; D.A. Dillman, *Mail and Telephone Surveys: The Total Design Method* (New York: Wiley, 1978), Chapter 3; also Oppenheim, *op. cit.*, Chapter 3; Moser and Kalton, *op. cit.*, Chapter 13.
20. Dillman, *op. cit.*
21. A.L. Edwards, *The Social Desirability Variable in Personality Assessment and Research* (New York: Dryden Press, 1957); S. Messick and J. Ross (eds.), *Measurement of Personality and Cognition* (New York: Wiley, 1962).
22. H.J. Eysenck, "Response Set, Authoritarianism, and Personality Questionnaires," *British Journal of Social and Clinical Psychology 3* (1964), pp. 216–25.
23. Moser and Kalton, *op. cit.*, Chapter 15.
24. Dillman, *op. cit.*, pp. 95–105.
25. Dunham and Smith, *op. cit.*, p. 82.

Chapter 4

ADMINISTRATION PROCEDURE

Similar to the planning and development of the survey process, administration and implementation procedures require a well-thought-out course of action. Some potential problems, such as failure to explain the instructions for completing the questionnaire clearly or not allowing enough time for employees to respond thoughtfully to the survey, may almost seem too trivial to mention. Other problems, such as the development of a cover letter that will convince people to respond fully and truthfully or the establishment of standardized conditions and procedures for administering the questionnaire, may seem more difficult. Failure to consider these aspects of the survey process, however, can render much of the data collected virtually useless. Indeed, no matter how much effort has gone into the preliminary diagnosis of organizational problems or the development and testing of the survey questionnaire, poor response often occurs because of "simple" problems that were not anticipated.

The Importance of Planning Ahead

Various aspects of the administration of an attitude survey require substantial advance planning. If a survey is to be conducted using an optical scanning procedure, for example, the development and printing of the response forms alone takes approximately six weeks. Allowing sufficient time for the development and testing of computer programs can facilitate the analysis and evaluation phase by preventing delays due to mistakes in the computer program. Other, often subtle, scheduling concerns must be considered as well. Summer months, for instance, are *not* usually good times to administer a survey because of the number of people on vacation and the resulting overload that is often placed on those at work. If the planning of the survey initially begins in the late winter or early spring, even something as obvious as vacation schedules might be overlooked. Thus a timetable that considers these factors and allows individuals within the organization to gain a clearer picture of the entire survey process is an important priority.

Although Chapter 4 is relatively brief, the failure to fully consider its contents can upset an otherwise well-planned survey. This chapter focuses on the timetable, promotion of the survey, development of the response forms, and administrative instructions and procedures.

Program Timetable

Based on the work in which we have been involved, a reasonable time period from the initiation of the survey process to the presentation of the final report to management and the participants is approximately six months. The major portion of this time should be focused on the initial phases of planning and development. In fact, some organizational researchers have even suggested that surveys should be scheduled one year in advance, particularly in large organizations.[1] This framework allows sufficient time to conduct sensing and polling sessions, to develop and pilot test the questionnaire, and to order necessary materials. Thus, the rationale underlying the formulation of a timetable is to plan for these various phases and other factors that require lead time, and for such considerations as summer vacations, holiday seasons, analysis time, and so forth.

A brief illustration can point out some of the time lags involved. On the first survey undertaken by the authors, the initial preparatory work began in late March. The survey itself was developed and reviewed during April and early May, and finally administered during the last week of May. Initial feedback of the preliminary analysis was presented in early July, and the final report was then completed in September, four months after the participants had taken part in the survey. By the time the survey results were publicized in a report to the participants, summer vacations had passed, and the survey itself seemed remote. At this point, employee reaction to the survey and its usefulness to the organization's management were not as favorable as they could have been.

Because early feedback provides people with information while issues are still fresh in their minds, subsequent surveys were planned so that the data collection process occurred during the late winter. Correspondingly, the analysis was to be completed one month from the time the data were collected. During these latter efforts, the entire process was completed before Memorial Day so that the results of the survey could be made public to the employees prior to the vacation season. The actual timetable for the most recent of the authors' survey feedback programs is presented in Table 4–1.

As indicated in this table, although the main survey work was completed within a six-month period, the bank used a number of follow-up groups composed of a cross section of its employee population to discuss the results of the survey and to make suggestions to management. In this instance, the process was thus extended to approximately one year. Utilization of such follow-up groups will be discussed in Chapter 5.

Introductory Letter: Why an Attitude Survey?

A brief introductory letter communicating the appeal of the survey and inviting employees to take part in the overall process is a useful part of the implementation procedure. This phase is especially important for initial assessment of employee opinions, for it serves to introduce the survey to the employee population and to motivate them to participate. Such a letter can also be used to provide information concerning when, where, and how the survey will be implemented. Since this letter is often the one opportunity the surveyors may have to reach some employees, it should anticipate and counter any questions concerning the study. Thus the letter should include specific pieces of information and yet not be too long to discourage potential respondents from reading it.

Depending on whether the entire organization or a sample (target) group is being surveyed, the introductory letter can take two different approaches. If the entire organization is to take part in the survey, the letter can be included in the house organ. If the survey is to be focused on a particular group of employees (for example, administrative support personnel), the letter should be sent directly to those who will be involved. If the latter course is chosen, the letter should be written on the organization's letterhead stationery. Regardless of the approach selected, the letter should focus on the following issues:

1. *Why the survey is being undertaken.* The answer may be as

Table 4-1 Survey Process Timetable

Time Frame	Activity	Phase of Cyclical Planned Intervention Model
1/18	Initial meeting between consultants and bank personnel officers Interviews with key bank officers and executives	Diagnosis/Development Phase: 1. Meetings with various personnel 2. Meetings with cross-sectional groups 3. Instrument design 4. Preparation of computer programs
2/21–26	Organization sensing sessions with following groups: 1. executive (assistant vice presidents and up) 2. supervisory employees 3. nonsupervisory employees	
2/29	Question and development session: consultants and personnel officers	
3/04	Final draft of the survey questionnaire prior to pilot testing	
3/05	Initial development of computer packages (adapted from Statistical Package for Social Sciences)	
3/06	Pilot test of survey questionnaire with a sample of bank personnel	
3/07	Training session for survey administrators	
3/10	Final questionnaire reproduced by printer	
3/18–20	Attitude survey administered bankwide	Implementation Phase: 1. Administration, collection of data 2. Preliminary data analysis 3. Initial feedback to clients
4/18	Preliminary analysis and initial report to participants prepared by consultants	
5/23	Final report to management prepared by consultants	Data Evaluation: 1. In-depth analysis 2. Oral and written reports (feedback) 3. Receipt of recommendations for action from follow-up groups 4. Development of action plans by department heads
6/15	Biweekly survey follow-up groups initiated by the organization	
12/1	Final report from follow-up groups	

simple as stating that the survey is part of an ongoing practice to keep the organization informed and up-to-date about employee concerns regarding their jobs and the firm. If the survey is being used in response to a specific set of issues, these should be pointed out. For introductory survey efforts, including a brief paragraph about the nature of attitude surveys and the types of questions respondents will be asked to answer can be useful.

2. *The use of sociodemographic data.*   As discussed in Chapter 3, most surveys include information concerning the respondent's job, work location, salary level, age, educational background, and so forth. Since respondents often have questions and potential fears as to how these data will be used, any concerns respondents may have should be alleviated by explaining that certain issues may be more important for specific segments of the organization than for others. Therefore, the organization needs to know how different groups of employees feel about certain issues. Thus, these data will *not* be used to identify individual employees, but rather to isolate important issues for particular groups in the organization.

3. *Confidentiality.*   Closely related to the use of sociodemographic data, the guarantee of both anonymity and confidentiality is an important aspect of the introductory letter. Part of the reason why employees do not respond truthfully to survey items is that they fear the data will be used in a punitive manner by the organization's management. Thus, assuring these individuals that they will not be identified in any way is important. When outside consultants are being used in the survey process, respondents can be assured that the consultants will be the only ones actually handling the raw data (questionnaires). The organization is only presented aggregations of response to the various issues included.

4. *Importance of participation.*   The letter should also convey to the employees that they are important to the successful implementation of the survey. Based on an assurance of confidentiality, potential respondents should be encouraged both to participate and to respond truthfully to the questions, making comments where appropriate.

5. *Use of results.*   Most employees will want to know how the data are going to be used. The letter provides a good opportunity to convey this information. In addition, it is useful to explain that such surveys are not panaceas to organizational problems, but that they can provide managers with a clearer picture of the nature and quality of employee work life. If the organization is planning to announce

the results of the survey to the employees, which is usually the practice, the organization should so inform the respondents that within a few weeks after the survey (using the timetable as a guide) they will receive a summary of the results.

6. *Logistics.* Finally, logistical information concerning when, where, and how the survey will be administered can be included in the introductory letter. Also, the employees should be given a rough idea of how long the survey will take.

A sample introductory letter used in one of our recent surveys is presented in Figure 4–1. Since the fact that an attitude survey is being considered or planned becomes organizational knowledge fairly quickly, the introductory letter should be made public early in the survey process. In fact, a good idea is to let as many people as possible in the organization or groups being targeted know about the survey and have the opportunity to give their input. Such publicity will not only stimulate thought about the survey, but also will provide employees with an increased sense of involvement.

Since the introductory letter is used fairly early in the survey process, we have found it useful for the organization's chief executive officer to send out a memorandum of encouragement shortly before the survey is administered. This memo serves to remind participants when the questionnaire will be implemented, and to lend top management support to the process. Such a memo should also reiterate the importance of the participation of all employees and the confidentiality of the data gathered. An example of a memo used in one of our recent surveys is presented in Figure 4–2.

Development of the Response Form

Basically, two different approaches can be employed for collecting the survey data. The first method is to have the respondents simply respond to the items directly on the questionnaire. The alternative procedure is to use an optical scanning form on which the respondents answer the questions by darkening the appropriate areas on the form. Each method has its own strengths and weaknesses and slightly different procedural steps.

In the optical scanning procedure, respondents answer the closed-ended questions on a specially designed scoring sheet with a No. 2 pencil. These sheets are similar to those used in the SAT college board examinations or other large, group-administered tests.

If open-ended questions (which require a sentence or two) are employed, respondents are instructed to answer them on a separate sheet of paper. By using identification numbers, these answers may be coded and merged with the closed-ended responses for analysis. When using this approach, care must be taken to avoid associating names with identification numbers to ensure confidentiality.

Optical scanning forms come in three basic styles: (1) "universal" forms, (2) "do-it-yourself" customized forms, and (3) professionally developed customized forms. The universal format, usually available through any university testing service, contains sufficient room for appropriate sociodemographic data and two hundred survey items, with each question having five possible alternatives. In one of the early surveys we administered, the universal form approach was used. However, because we had difficulty developing clear instructions for this form, we decided in a later survey to develop a customized form, which better reflected the organization's needs and identity.

If the customized format approach is chosen, planning must begin early in the survey process, for developing and reprinting tailor-made forms takes at least six weeks. You can either put the format together yourself or have an outside organization develop the forms professionally.* The "do-it-yourself" approach that we used was less expensive than the professionally developed format, and the results were satisfactory. However, a typeset form is clearly neater and more professional-looking than a typewritten piece. In our opinion the money saved was not worth the difficulty or the aggravation. Also, keep in mind that if your organization plans to make such a process a biennial management practice, the same basic format can be used during subsequent survey efforts, thus making the professionally prepared form affordable. An example of such a form is provided in Figure 4–3. Before submitting forms for optical scanning, they must be checked for stray marks and erasures. Since the scanning machine picks up all marks on the response form, uncleaned stray marks may distort the final data used for analysis. Even though the instructions may have clearly indicated that the answers should consist of a heavy black mark between the two lines reserved for the particular response selected by the individual, mistakes are virtually inevitable. In past surveys we have conducted, for exam-

---

* The company we have used in our survey operations is Data Forms of National Computer System, 197 F. Greenfield Road, Lancaster, Pennsylvania 17601.

Figure 4–1   Sample Introductory Letter

Why an Attitude Survey?

An attitude survey, sometimes called a quality of work life survey, is a questionnaire process that gathers information about employee opinions. From an employee's point of view, it provides an opportunity to tell the organization what he or she wants it to know in an anonymous, confidential way. Questions on the survey have been developed from issues expressed during discussions with small groups of employees throughout the bank. Most of these questions are put in statement form with a "strongly agree—strongly disagree" framework. Other questions are better served by open-ended responses that are written out, such as the things an individual likes or dislikes about the bank. Some issues were raised in the small group discussions that were too complex or involved to be asked of a large number of employees. These concerns have been summarized and forwarded directly to top management.

Other issues are important for only certain sections of the bank, or for certain groups. To this end, the initial questions that ask you to identify your job cluster, your salary level, your racial background, your sex, and your occupational location allow the researchers to identify particular issues that are of concern to some but not all employees. For instance, it is important for the bank to know that one job cluster may not feel adequately trained for the job, but that other job clusters feel differently. If this were the case, training programs could then be set up which could help with that particular problem.

The success of an attitude survey depends on everyone's *full participation*, as well as keeping individual responses *strictly confidential*. Neither the bank nor the researchers have any interest in knowing how individuals respond to the questionnaire. Quite frankly, we are looking for those things you feel the bank does well and those things that need improvement.

While an attitude survey is helpful in finding out what people are thinking, it is not a "cure all." There are, of course, other ways of assessing what employees think about certain issues. If an attitude survey *and* another source of information, such as complaints, the "grapevine," or informal discussions, identify the same issues as either a problem area or an area of high satisfaction, then the bank can be reasonably certain that it has identified an important issue. In the bank's case, the number of personnel has increased in the past two years. Moreover, thrift institutions have been controlled by Regulation Q interest ceilings. These have created economic complexities in this time of high inflation. Thus, savings banks are under external constraints that can have a significant influence on people's feelings about their working and nonworking lives. To this end, a number of questions ask for your basis of response for a particular question. For example, if your response concerning certain types of benefits is based on benefits at (organization's name), this gives management a different problem to solve than if the basis of your response is outside the bank.

In brief, attitude surveys can alert management to trends in employee opinions. Management then has some choices to make in addressing these issues. They may choose to make some changes outright; for other issues they may decide to use follow-up groups in the same manner as the last survey. Since some issues are controlled by forces outside the bank, however, the bank has to work through professional groups, such as the local Savings Bank Association, to change legislation or turn the situation around in other ways. Thus, in cases of external problems, it is useful for the bank to know the feelings of its employees to build a case for changes needed outside of the immediate control of an individual bank. To these ends, an attitude survey can be a useful method of obtaining important information as part of the internal and external change process.

The attitude survey will be administered in _____ during the following times:

_____

_____

_____

The questionnaire will take approximately 30 minutes to complete. After you have completed the survey, it will be deposited in a locked "ballot box," which will be forwarded to the consultants at (*organizational affiliation*).

If you cannot attend any of the above times, provisions will be made for a sealed envelope to be forwarded to you with a return envelope addressed to (*consultant*) at (*organizational affiliation*). Once again, we urge you to participate in this survey.

Figure 4-2   Sample CEO Reminder

MEMORANDUM #76–80
TO: All Employees
FROM: (The Bank President)
RE: 1980 Attitude Survey

The 1980 Employees' Attitude Survey will be administered on *Tuesday, March 18, Wednesday, March 19, and Thursday, March 20.*

An attitude survey acts as a communication vehicle from employees to the chief executive officer. It gives you an opportunity to express YOUR feelings and opinions concerning various bank policies and practices. Those employees who were with the bank when the last survey was administered (March 1978) will remember questions regarding advancement, pay, the job, equal employment opportunity, the supervisor, relationships with co-workers, working conditions, and the bank in general. By responding to issues such as these, the bank is able to develop a profile of staff attitudes to determine, in a systematic way, how you, as a part of a *group*, feel about the working environment at (the bank). The results will indicate general areas of employee feelings along several dimensions.

To ensure confidentiality, the survey will be conducted by Professors James Bowditch of Boston College and Anthony Buono of Bentley College. We ask you to be candid in your responses. An individual's responses to the survey will not be identified. Survey results will be reported in group responses that will assure anonymity. Your input into the survey is *completely confidential!*

In mid-February, cross sections of bank employees met with members of the Personnel Department and Professors Bowditch and Buono to discuss bank-related issues for possible inclusion in this year's survey. These meetings proved meaningful and gave greater insight into the working environment at the bank. The ideas and issues presented will help to make our 1980 survey relevant.

The findings will be mailed to your home address approximately 6 weeks after the survey is administered.

The bank is committed to follow up survey results. A follow-up group will be established to review the results and make recommendations to management.

Your participation is not only fully appreciated, but also necessary if this effort is to be meaningful.

March 5, 1980

Figure 4-3 Sample Response Sheet

MEDIUM SIZED SAVINGS BANK

EMPLOYEE OPINION AND ATTITUDE SURVEY

Background Information

1 Group Classification   a b c d e f g h i j k l m n o p

2 Salary Classification   a b c d e f g h i

3 Age Group   a b c d e f g h i j

4 Length of Employment   a b c d e f g h

5 Previous Full-Time Jobs   a b c d e   8 Sex   a b

6 Education   a b c d e   9 Race   a b

7 Job Cluster   a b c d e f g   10 a b c

Questions

1 a b c d e f	31 a b c d e f	61 a b c d e f	91 a b c d e f
2 a b c d e f	32 a b c d e f	62 a b c d e f	92 a b c d e f
3 a b c d e f	33 a b c d e f	63 a b c d e f	93 a b c d e f
4 a b c d e f	34 a b c d e f	64 a b c d e f	94 a b c d e f
5 a b c d e f	35 a b c d e f	65 a b c d e f	95 a b c d e f
6 a b c d e f	36 a b c d e f	66 a b c d e f	96 a b c d e f
7 a b c d e f	37 a b c d e f	67 a b c d e f	97 a b c d e f
8 a b c d e f	38 a b c d e f	68 a b c d e f	98 a b c d e f
9 a b c d e f	39 a b c d e f	69 a b c d e f	99 a b c d e f
10 a b c d e f	40 a b c d e f	70 a b c d e f	100 a b c d e f
11 a b c d e f	41 a b c d e f	71 a b c d e f	
12 a b c d e f	42 a b c d e f	72 a b c d e f	
13 a b c d e f	43 a b c d e f	73 a b c d e f	
14 a b c d e f	44 a b c d e f	74 a b c d e f	
15 a b c d e f	45 a b c d e f	75 a b c d e f	
16 a b c d e f	46 a b c d e f	76 a b c d e f	
17 a b c d e f	47 a b c d e f	77 a b c d e f	
18 a b c d e f	48 a b c d e f	78 a b c d e f	
19 a b c d e f	49 a b c d e f	79 a b c d e f	
20 a b c d e f	50 a b c d e f	80 a b c d e f	
21 a b c d e f	51 a b c d e f	81 a b c d e f	
22 a b c d e f	52 a b c d e f	82 a b c d e f	
23 a b c d e f	53 a b c d e f	83 a b c d e f	
24 a b c d e f	54 a b c d e f	84 a b c d e f	
25 a b c d e f	55 a b c d e f	85 a b c d e f	
26 a b c d e f	56 a b c d e f	86 a b c d e f	
27 a b c d e f	57 a b c d e f	87 a b c d e f	
28 a b c d e f	58 a b c d e f	88 a b c d e f	
29 a b c d e f	59 a b c d e f	89 a b c d e f	
30 a b c d e f	60 a b c d e f	90 a b c d e f	

ple, respondents have circled rather than darkened in the appro-priate spaces. Others have drummed their pencils on the sheet, leaving marks which, if unerased, could mislead the optical scanner. Still others have used pens, which are not read by the optical scan-ner, instead of No. 2 pencils. These are simply *some* of the potential problems that can emerge with this approach. The time involved in editing and cleaning the data is, thus, a critical part of the process.

The second alternative to collecting the survey data is to develop the questionnaire so that respondents can answer the questions di-rectly on the instrument. Depending on the capabilities of the com-puter system, the data are then keypunched directly onto computer cards or tape. Although this approach has the advantage of allowing the researchers to check the data more readily and of eliminating the need for separate answer sheets for open-ended questions, keypunching is a laborious manual task. Not only does it require a longer period of time than optical scanning, but when used for more than 250 respondents, it is more expensive as well.

The key to this approach is to develop a questionnaire with re-sponse spaces and keypunching instructions directly on the instru-ment. This approach also provides a convenient way to intermingle open-ended questions with the closed-ended ones. If this is done, these written responses can be coded directly on the sheet and keypunched with the closed-ended data. Thus, all questions can be analyzed at the same time rather than having to create and merge two separate files, as is required by the optical scanning procedure. Moreover, personal identification numbers, which often make re-spondents uncomfortable about being identified, are not needed since the responses are all included in the same form. A sample format is provided in Figure 4–4.

Once the data are collected and fed into the computer, the analy-sis process is the same for both approaches. To keep the time lag to a minimum, regardless of the approach employed, the procedure and computer programs should be checked before the data are collected. This step is accomplished by simply filling out ten to fifteen optical scanning or questionnaire forms, scanning or keypunching them as required, and creating a "dummy" file. This process can simplify the analysis phase since any potential interruption in "debugging" the scanning procedure or computer programs can be minimized. Thus, lengthy time loss after the data are collected can be avoided.

Figure 4-4 Sample Direct Response Answer Sheet

The answer scale is as follows:

1 = Strongly agree	5 = Strongly disagree
2 = Agree	6 = I do not understand
3 = Neutral (neither agree	the question
nor disagree)	7 = Not applicable
4 = Disagree	

- -

22. My [research lab] benefits are good. (If disagree, state why.) ——

1/52

_____

_____

_____

53-54

22a. The basis for my response to the preceding question is: ——

55

1. Benefits at [research lab]
2. Benefits compared to [nearby university]
3. Benefits outside [research lab and nearby university]
4. My own sense of a good benefit plan

23. [Research lab] policy and procedure changes are made available to me on a timely basis. ____

56

24. My supervisor really understands the complexities of my job. ____

57

25. There is good *COMMUNICATION* (including feedback) within [research lab]. (If disagree, please state why.) ____

58

_____

_____

_____

59-60

26. There are enough administrative support personnel in my division to do the job well. ____

61

27. Favoritism plays no part in job promotions. ____

62

28. I think my work space is sufficient. ____

63

29. The Travel Office is cooperative. ____

64

30. I think the laboratory hires well qualified administrative support people. ____

65

Development of Instructions

Instructions on how to complete the survey must be done with as much care as the development of the questionnaire itself. Moreover, before they are actually used in the survey process, instructions should be pilot tested for clarity and potential misunderstanding. Even in the most favorable situation, for example, when a researcher is present during the administration of the survey, respondents may feel embarrassed about asking procedural questions. If a sufficient number of employees experience subsequent difficulty in taking the survey, the data gathered could be so distorted as to be rendered useless. For those respondents with poor reading skills, it may even be necessary to have a neutral third party aid them in filling out the questionnaire.

Two examples of instruction sheets are presented in Figures 4–5 and 4–6. The first was used for an optical scanning procedure. The second was developed for an integrated questionnaire with the responses placed directly on the survey itself. Although each instruction form has its own unique aspects, they both begin with an introduction to the survey and a sample question with its possible responses. The instructions then inform the respondent *how* the items on the survey should be answered. For surveys utilizing the optical scanning procedure, we have found that having an administrator show people how to fill in the response areas on a blackboard or a flip chart facilitates the cleaning and editing process.

Instructions that describe in detail how the sociodemographic data should be recorded are included as well. Issues of job classification, salary classification, job location, age, race, sex, and other items of potential interest are treated here. In one of the surveys we conducted, the bank's management felt that some of the respondents might not know their salary classification. Thus, each respondent was given a separate card with his or her name and that information on it and instructed to use it to respond to the appropriate question (see Figure 4–5).

The second set of instructions presented in Figure 4–6 were developed for a format where responses were placed directly on the questionnaire. Although the basic information is the same as in the preceding example, it is presented differently and includes other kinds of information as well. Under each response space, for instance, there is a code (for example, 1/16, 2/34, etc.). These numbers

Figure 4–5 Sample Instructions for Optical Scanning Forms

ATTITUDE SURVEY—INSTRUCTIONS

The following is a questionnaire designed to get at attitudes related to your work at the bank. In the development of this survey, a wide cross section of individuals created questions or raised issues for possible inclusion. Some of your co-workers spent an evening engaged in this task. The result is the questionnaire that you are asked to complete.

Most of the issues are in statement form.

Example: The bank is an enjoyable place to work.
  a. Strongly agree
  b. Agree
  c. Neutral—neither agree nor disagree or no opinion
  d. Disagree
  e. Strongly disagree
  f. I do not understand the question

Some issues will follow a slightly different format. In these cases, the entire statement with possible responses will be presented.

You are asked to respond in the following way. Make a mark with the No. 2 pencil in the space corresponding to the answer you choose to give to the statement. If, for example, you *agreed* that the bank was an enjoyable place to work, but not strongly agreed, you would darken in the "b" slot for that question. We have also included a page of open-ended questions on which we would like your comments. While we are looking for *your feelings* (not the bank's) about issues, if you do not think you have enough information to express an opinion, let us know on the separate, open-ended answer sheet.

One final, introductory remark—these surveys are to be kept confidential. While we wish to know what kind of job you have, and your salary classification, we *do not* want to know who you are. Quite frankly, we are looking for those things you think we, as a bank, are doing well, and those things we need to improve. To ensure confidentiality, the questions will be analyzed by professional survey researchers at Boston College.

Below are the job, salary, and other classification data we need. Instructions follow on how to fill in the classification data on both the computerized and open-ended answer sheets.

Since we do not want to identify anyone, *please do not put your name on the answer sheets.* While it is important that you answer all questions to assure the survey gives a complete picture, *you may omit any questions you feel uncomfortable about.* IMPORTANT: For questions 2 and 7, the survey administrator will give you an index card with all pertinent information and respective codes.

---

1. The first row indicates work classifications. Also *write* this answer in the space provided on the "open-ended answer sheet" next to #1-Work Group Classification.

   Retail:
   a. Group I
   b. Group II
   c. Group III
   d. Savings Services, NOW Department, and Retail Administration

   Lending:
   e. Residential Lending, Commercial Lending, and Loan Administration.
   f. Loan Servicing
   g. Credit Adjustment and Credit Organization

   Finance and Control:
   h. Accounting, Finance & Control Administration, and Office of the President
   i. EDP Control and Audit
   j. SBLI and Community Affairs

   Administration and Support:
   k. Building
   l. Purchasing (including Messengers, Switchboard, and Stockroom)
   m. Personnel, Administrative and Support, and Microfilm
   n. Marketing (includes Business Development)

2. In the second row, please mark your salary classification (refer to index card):
   a. = Part Time
   b. = Class I
   c. = Class II
   d. = Class III
   e. = Class IV
   f. = Class V
   g. = Class VI
   h. = Class VII
   i. = Class VIII and above

3. In row three, your age:

a. = 18–20	d. = 31–35	g. = 46–50	j. = 61–70
b. = 21–25	e. = 36–40	h. = 51–55	
c. = 26–30	f. = 41–45	i. = 56–60	

4. Length of present employment at the bank: Also *write* this answer in the space provided on the "open-ended answer sheet" next to #2—Length of Employment.

    a. = Less than 6 months
    b. = More than 6 months but less than 1 year
    c. = More than 1 year but less than 3 years
    d. = More than 3 years but less than 5 years
    e. = More than 5 years but less than 10 years
    f. = More than 10 years but less than 15 years
    g. = More than 15 years but less than 20 years
    h. = 20 years and over

5. Number of your previous full-time jobs:
    a. = None
    b. = 1
    c. = 2
    d. = 3
    e. = 4 or more

6. Your education level: Also *write* this answer in the space provided on the "open-ended answer sheet" next to #3—Level of Education.
    a. = Less than high school
    b. = High school graduate
    c. = Some college
    d. = College graduate
    e. = Graduate school

7. In the seventh row, please mark your job cluster (refer to index card): Also *write* this answer in the space provided on the "open-ended answer sheet" next to #4—Job Cluster.
    a. = Teller
    b. = Head Teller/CSR
    c. = Operational/Clerical
    d. = Assistant Branch Manager/Branch Manager
    e. = Secretarial
    f. = Professional or Supervisory
    g. = Department Head/Assistant Manager
    h. = Assistant Division Head/Division Head

8. Your sex: a. = Male   b. = Female

9. Your race: a. = Nonminority   b. = Minority

Before you begin the Attitude Survey, please give the survey administrator the index card. It is a bookkeeping device to assure that everyone has received an Attitude Survey.

Are there any questions before you start? We hope you will find this questionnaire interesting. Thank you for your cooperation.

Figure 4–6 Sample Instructions for Response on Questionnaire Format

RESEARCH LABORATORY SUPPORT PERSONNEL
ATTITUDE SURVEY INSTRUCTIONS

The following is a questionnaire designed to get at attitudes related to your work at the laboratory. In the development of this survey, a random selection of individuals and other concerned people created questions or raised issues for possible inclusion. Some of your co-workers spent several afternoons engaged in this task. The result is the questionnaire that you are asked to complete.

Most issues are in statement form and call for the following responses:

Example:

1 = Strongly agree
2 = Agree
3 = Neutral (neither agree nor disagree)
4 = Disagree
5 = Strongly disagree
6 = I do not understand the question
7 = Not applicable

The laboratory is an enjoyable place to work.   2
                                                               ‾‾‾‾
                                                               1/16

You are asked to respond in the following way. Place the number (1 through 7) which corresponds to the response you choose for a particular question in the blank provided on the right-hand side of the statement. If, for example, you *agree* that the laboratory is an enjoyable place to work, but you do not strongly agree, you would place a "2" in the blank for that question. The number underneath the blank (in the example given above, 1/16) represents the IBM card and column number. These are instructions to the keypuncher and can be ignored.

Some issues will follow a slightly different format. In these cases, the entire statement with possible responses will be presented. We have also included a number of open-ended questions on which we would like your comments. While the questionnaire is focused toward getting at your feelings about certain issues, these open-ended questions give you an additional opportunity to express your opinion.

One final introductory remark—these surveys are to be kept *confidential*. While we wish to know what kind of job you have, your salary grade, how long you have been working for the laboratory, and so forth, we *do not* want to know who you are. Quite frankly, we are looking for those things you feel the laboratory is doing well and those things that need improvement. Since the success of the survey depends on your honest views, we urge you to be candid in your responses. To ensure confidentiality, the questions will be analyzed by professional survey researchers from Boston College and Bentley College.

The first part of the questionnaire includes salary, job, and other classification items. Instructions are provided on how to fill in these classification data on your survey form.

Since we do not want to identify anyone, *please do not put your name on the survey form.* While it is important that you answer all questions to ensure that the survey gives a complete picture, you may omit any questions you feel uncomfortable about.

Before you begin, if you have any questions, please discuss them with a survey administrator. We hope that you will find this questionnaire interesting.

LABORATORY SUPPORT PERSONNEL ATTITUDE SURVEY QUESTIONS

Unless otherwise indicated, place the letter that corresponds to your response in the space provided to the right of each question.

1. How long have you been working at the laboratory?   _____
                                                          1/06
    a. Less than 6 months
    b. More than 6 months but less than 1 year
    c. More than 1 year but less than 3 years
    d. More than 3 years but less than 5 years
    e. More than 5 years but less than 7 years
    f. More than 7 years but less than 10 years
    g. 10 years or more

2. How long have you been working in your present position?   _____
                                                                07
    a. Less than 6 months
    b. More than 6 months but less than 1 year
    c. More than 1 year but less than 3 years
    d. More than 3 years but less than 5 years
    e. More than 5 years but less than 7 years
    f. More than 7 years but less than 10 years
    g. 10 years or more

REMEMBER: ALL RESPONSES TO THIS SURVEY ARE STRICTLY CONFIDENTIAL.

3. What is your department number? (Please fill in the appropriate number only, for example: 20, 30, etc.)
                                                          _____
                                                          08–09

4. What is your job classification and grade? (e.g., Sec. II, Clerk IV, Computer Operator IV, etc.) _____
                                                          10–11

5. How many people do you work for directly? (Please fill in the appropriate number in terms of the ratio of secretarial/

administrative support personnel to people worked for. If, for example, there are 3 secretaries in your area and they work for 15 people, this would be a 1 to 5 ratio. You would then fill in a 5 in the space provided.)

_____
12–13

6. How many people do *you* directly supervise? (Please fill in the appropriate number.)

_____
14–15

7. How many people directly supervise you? (Please fill in the appropriate number.)

_____
16–17

8. How many people complete your performance evaluation? (Please fill in the appropriate number.)

_____
18–19

9. How old are you?

_____
1/20

   a. 20 or younger
   b. 21–25
   c. 26–30
   d. 31–35
   e. 36–40
   f. 41–45
   g. 46–55
   h. 56 and over

10. Your sex?

_____
21

   a. Male   b. Female

11. Your race?

_____
22

   a. Minority   b. Nonminority

12. What is your level of education?

_____
23

   a. Less than high school
   b. High school graduate
   c. Secretarial or technical school
   d. Some college/currently attending college
   e. College graduate
   f. Graduate school

13. Are you employed on a part-time or full-time basis?

_____
24

   a. Part-time   b. Full-time

are used to assist the keypuncher in placing the responses in the correct column of the hollarith (keypunch data) card, or data tape. The first digit indicates the card number, and the second indicates the appropriate column or columns to be employed.

In addition to the sample question and sociodemographic data, instructions should also remind respondents of the confidentiality of the survey. Since one of the keys to a successful survey is the assurance of anonymity, this is critical. As argued previously, if personnel think that they will be identified, their responses may reflect what they think the organization wants to hear and not what they actually think and feel.

Administration of the Survey

The actual administration of the survey can be handled in a number of different ways. One approach is to administer the survey during working hours in which several "sittings" over a one- to three-day period (depending on the size of the population) are scheduled. This is usually done in the organization's conference room. Either external consultants or in-house personnel trained in survey administration can be used to proctor the sessions. A second approach is to distribute the questionnaire at work with return envelopes to be mailed directly to the outside consultants. This approach is fairly costly in terms of postage. Moreover, if respondents have any questions concerning the survey, they cannot be readily answered. Experience has also shown that this approach generates a lower percentage of return than on-site administration. The third approach is to handle the entire process directly by mail. Again, in addition to added postage expense, the returns are proportionately less.

Overall, we have a distinct preference for on-site administration of the survey. The obvious advantages are (1) a far greater response rate than if the instrument is taken away from the organization to be completed at home, and (2) avoidance of postage costs and problems associated with the mail, although there are costs associated with taking work time to complete a survey. Furthermore, there is much less chance of contamination from other potential respondents—that is, with mail-in responses groups of employees often discuss the questions and decide how they will respond as a group to the various items. The result can be biased data for the researchers.

An appropriate procedure for an organization with a number of branch locations is to cluster administrative sites in relatively central locations. If the branches are large enough, the survey can be administered at each site. In one banking organization we have surveyed, the survey was given in three central branch locations and a central office location. Each branch location covered about five separate offices that were reasonably nearby. A number of surveys were left in each location for personnel to complete. Once persons had completed a survey, they would leave the instrument in a locked box, much like a paper ballot box. The researchers then gathered the completed surveys at the various locations and took them back to their offices at the university in preparation for the editing.

In another instance, the researchers conducted attitude surveys for an organization that was located in two large buildings. In this situation, as might be expected, the survey was given in one central location with one of the researchers in attendance. Having a central location simplified the procedure; administrators did not have to be trained, and the data could be prepared for analysis immediately following working hours on the days the surveys were administered.

One organization, particularly concerned that everyone have an opportunity to answer the survey, administered the questionnaire on site but mailed it to persons who were out sick or on vacation. Included in the packet was a mailer direct to the researchers, not the organization that was doing the survey. This, of course, helped to keep the procedure confidential and thus increased its credibility to the participants.

Training Survey Administrators·

If the on-site approach is selected, survey administrators should be fully knowledgeable about how to present the instructions to the participants and how to oversee the implementation process. Usually these individuals give the respondents a brief preliminary introduction to the survey and highlight the instructions. The administrator should then remain in the same place in the room, usually at the front or back, and provide assistance when requested to clarify the instructions or answer any questions the participants may have. Survey administrators should *not* circulate around the room or create the impression they are observing the people filling out the questionnaires.

Either the survey consultants or in-house personnel can be used as administrators. Employing an outsider in this role can avoid many problems. In many instances, organizations will choose to have the consultants themselves implement and administer the survey. When organizations prefer to use in-house personnel for administration purposes, caution must be taken to ensure that different administrators follow the same guidelines and do not intervene in the process. Although this point may seem overstated, ignoring it can bias the data being gathered.

In one survey, for example, a bank chose to have internal personnel oversee administration of the survey. Even though these individuals were trained and instructed on how to implement the survey, one of the administrators deviated from these guidelines. This person circulated around the room, checking to see if employees were filling in their responses on the optical scanning answer form in the appropriate manner. This tactic so unnerved some of the respondents that they omitted answering a number of sensitive questions.

The administrator is also responsible for collecting the questionnaires once the respondents have finished and have deposited their answer sheets in a locked box. The primary interest is to ensure anonymity of response. As respondents complete the survey, their response forms can be placed in individual folders and deposited in a locked "ballot" box by the respondent. The consultants then can go to the different administration centers to collect the information. Thus, no internal personnel handle any of the data—a process well accepted by employees.

If there are any doubts about the duties of the persons who are to assist in administering the survey, having a practice session to clear up any ambiguities is a good idea. No one, of course, can anticipate all of the questions a person is likely to ask about procedural issues, but the survey administrators can be given some tough procedural questions to answer as a means of getting prepared for the actual survey conditions.

Summary

This chapter began with a focus on the importance of planning ahead. As we complete our discussion of the administration phase of the survey-based approach we propose, we must reiterate the importance of comprehensive planning and thinking through administrative procedures. Even if the response forms have been carefully developed, and even if the instructions have been pilot tested and found to be clear and explicit, a number of problems can still emerge, and biases in the data can still arise. Thus, the entire administration process must be monitored to ensure uniformity in the ways in which questionnaires are disseminated and data are collected to minimize these potential difficulties.

Although the ideas discussed in this chapter might seem somewhat routine, many surveys have overlooked some of these concerns. Considering the time, effort, and expense extended to develop an effective quality of work life assessment, having the process undermined by ineffective administration procedures is a needless waste. For an organization to ensure that the data to be analyzed and acted upon are meaningful and valid, sufficient time and effort must be given to these more mundane, "routine" matters.

Endnote

1. R. Dunham and F. Smith, *Organizational Surveys: An Internal Assessment of Organizational Health* (Glenview, Ill.: Scott, Foresman, 1979), pp. 85–86.

Chapter 5

DATA ANALYSIS AND EVALUATION

Although the planning and development of organizational surveys are the keys to comprehensive assessments of the quality of working life, data analysis and interpretation are critical to lucid feedback to management and employees. Indeed, if quality of work life surveys are to be useful to organizations, they must reflect thoughtful planning, execution, *and* analysis of the information gathered. Of course, while no sophisticated analytic technique can overcome a badly planned and executed survey, the formulation of a comprehensive procedure for the analysis of the data is essential for a timely and meaningful assessment.

The analysis phase begins once the data from the survey have been gathered. The process entails the editing and coding of the data, the analysis itself, interpretation of the results, and finally, preparation of the report and feedback of the results. Although Chapter 5 will follow this sequence, the reverse order is more useful when actually designing quality of work life surveys. By considering the kinds of information an organization's management would like to see included in the final report, the researchers can more fully establish the requirements for analysis, interpretation, and the coding and editing procedures.[1] Thus, ensuring that the analysis reflects those issues that are of concern to an organization's management means establishing these procedures early in the survey process. To do so will minimize delays and other problems with this phase.

Editing the Data

Once the data have been collected, they must be carefully edited before coding and analysis can begin. Whether the survey employs optical scanning forms or questionnaires with appropriate spaces for responses, editing is intended to detect and eliminate errors in the completed survey. Although this task is routine and therefore a repetitive and dull undertaking, it is a necessary step to keep to a minimum the errors that inevitably creep into the process. Considering the time and effort that have gone into the survey process to this point, having a thorough analysis defeated by simple mistakes in the data makes no sense.

The editing itself depends on the type of response form employed, and these forms must be checked prior to coding and analysis for completeness, accuracy, and uniformity.[2]

Although participants are usually informed that they can omit any question or set of questions they wish, they should also be encouraged to respond to all the items to ensure that the survey provides the organization with as complete a perspective as possible. Thus, the first point in editing is to check that there is a response to each item on the questionnaire. While inevitably some data in the survey will be missing, any questionnaire that has an excessive number of omissions should be excluded from the analysis. Unfortunately, there are no set rules underlying this decision; rather, such guidelines should be established by the survey professionals and applied in a consistent manner.[3]

By keeping track of omissions to specific questions, sensitive areas may also be identified. If, for example, a number of respondents did not answer one or two of the same questions, the lack of response could point to a controversial issue. People usually leave a question blank when they disagree with it or are critical of the issue or are concerned that their response could be used against them. Thus, a high degree of nonresponse can indicate a low level of trust in the organization.

For closed-ended questions, when optical scanning forms are used, the person doing the editing should also check for stray marks and extraneous responses. As discussed in the previous chapter, these marks can readily mislead the scanner as it "reads" the results. When responses are included directly on the questionnaire, the editor should check that all numbers or letters are clearly marked to facilitate the keypunching process.

It is much more difficult to check for completeness in open-ended responses. The main effort in this instance should be to ensure that the responses are legible for the coders and that the responses make sense—that is, the meaning of the response is clear.

Even though they may be instructed to select only one alternative per question, respondents often choose more than one answer for a particular question. This type of inaccuracy may be due to carelessness or to a conscious attempt to provide misleading answers. If a number of such double-responses appear on a particular questionnaire, as with an incomplete survey, that questionnaire should be omitted from the analysis.

Other potential errors include recording the responses in the wrong places, circling rather than darkening in responses on optical scanning forms, writing in responses to closed-ended questions rather than using the appropriate codes, and so forth. Although not all of these response errors can always be caught, they can be minimized through a careful editing of each questionnaire or optical scanning response form; the actual scanning or keypunching of the data will proceed much more easily and efficiently.

The editing phase of the survey process also provides an opportunity to check whether respondents have correctly interpreted questions and instructions in a uniform manner. In some instances, depending on the response to the previous question or the individual's position in the organization, a particular question might not be applicable to a respondent. In one of our surveys, for example, a bank had recently undergone a reorganization to divisions, and the bank's management was interested in finding out how employees who had been with the bank prior to the restructuring perceived the divisional move. Respondents were instructed to answer that particular question *only* if they had been employed before a certain date. In such instances, it is important to ensure that individuals who do not meet the "criteria" for a particular question record the correct "not applicable" response and not a misleading answer.

One question that often emerges is whether all or only a sample of the surveys should be edited. Again, no general rule can be given since the decision essentially depends on balancing the probability of various errors in the data with the time and effort required by careful editing. On the one hand, spending a lot of time on a full edit is not an efficient use of one's resources if the errors corrected are relatively minor and if the complete editing would entail devoting less attention to potentially more important phases of the survey process. On the other hand, a sample check, by providing an opportunity to correct errors in the questionnaires selected, is more useful as an indicator of the quality of the data rather than as an error-correcting procedure. If the questionnaires are unlikely to contain many errors, a useful approach is to perform an initial quality check for uniformity, followed by a complete computer edit.

If the data are to be analyzed by computer, the computer itself is an extremely useful device in editing for uniformity since it can provide a complete and thorough check on the data in its final form, just prior to analysis. One method is simply to check that all responses fall within their correct ranges. For instance, if respondents' sex is coded male as 0 and female as 1, then a response that is either keypunched or read through the optical scanner as a 6 would be an obvious error. A second approach in computer editing is to look at the internal consistency between responses. Often some questions are oriented only toward certain groups of employees (for example, tellers, supervisors, and so forth). These questions should, of course, be answered only by the appropriate group. Similarly, improbable combinations of responses can also be detected through detailed checking. For instance, an employee who falls in the lowest salary classification is unlikely to have been working for the organization for a relatively long period of time. Through simple cross-tabulation, data such as these can be checked for their consistency and uniformity.

In summary, the extent and complexity of the editing process depends on the type of response form employed, scoring procedures that are adopted, and policies that are formulated to handle missing data, incomplete questionnaires, and inconsistent responses. Although no set guidelines exist and the procedures used must be adapted to the particular survey in question, survey administrators must ensure that a uniform policy is established and followed to minimize distortion in the data.

Coding

Before data can actually be analyzed, they must be scored or coded according to a set format. For questions with a closed-ended response continuum (for example, responses ranging from "strongly agree" to "strongly disagree"), this process is relatively simple and usually accomplished during the development of the questionnaire (for example, "strongly agree" = 5, "agree" = 4, "neutral" = 3, and so on). The important point is to ensure that coding formats are uniform. As discussed above, preparing the data for analysis also entails making sure that there is only one response per question, that responses are accurate, and that instructions have been consistently followed.

Open-ended questions, by contrast, require a more extensive coding procedure. The basic purpose of coding these open-ended questions is to classify the responses into meaningful categories that bring out their essential patterns. *Coding frames* that reflect the range of responses given must be developed for specific questions. One approach to this type of coding is referred to as *content analysis*, a systematic analysis and description of the content of the information provided by the respondents. The terms "coding" and "content analysis" are often used interchangeably since they reflect the same basic process. In practice, however, *coding* is usually applied to research data and *content analysis* for materials that exist in the everyday course of events such as newspapers, magazines, and so forth. Newspapers, for example, may be studied to determine the changing attention given to certain political or community issues over a specific time period; the content of different papers over time can then be compared to bring out differing attitudes toward certain issues and their evolution.[4] As a process, content analysis will be delineated more fully in the discussion of qualitative data analysis.

The coding of open-ended questions essentially involves two basic steps: (1) a decision on the categories to be used and (2) the allocation of individual responses to these different categories. In some instances, such coding may take two or more sortings. In other words, if a question that seeks global dislikes about the job produces a large number of complaints about salary, a second sort through the same question may attempt to categorize the *types* of complaints about the salary. An important consideration in this type of coding is to be as concise and clear as possible. In early coding, it is advisable to retain more rather than less detail since integrating different categories together during data analysis is much simpler than splitting one grouping into several groups when the categories have been coded alike. The trade-off is to avoid extensive coding that makes the analysis too unwieldy and results in an inability to allocate answers to different categories accurately. In such data summarization, retaining too many categories is just as misleading as employing too few.

Coding of open-ended questions is a time-consuming and expensive process. Thus, such questions should be selected with care. Moreover, when there are large numbers of such questions and responses, the survey administrators may decide to take a random or stratified sample of those questions for coding and then generalize to the population of survey responses.

If open-ended questions are interspersed with closed-ended questions throughout the survey, the content analysis or coding of the open-ended questions should be accomplished prior to keypunching to facilitate the analysis phase of the work. In optical scanning types of questionnaires, analysis can begin on the closed-ended question data while the coding of the open-ended questions is ongoing. The two sets of information can then be merged during the actual reporting of the data.

A brief, final word about coding is necessary. Since the type of information generated by open-ended questions in organizational surveys is rarely highly personal in nature, much of the coding is usually straightforward. However, even assuming a clear and concise coding frame, coding itself is rarely a matter of automatically applying set rules. In many instances, the coder will have to exercise judgment on doubtful answers. In these situations, the possibility of personal bias and differences across coders presents a potential analytic bias. One way to minimize such bias is to have different individuals "double-code" a sample of questions analyzed by others. By comparing the two sets of results, this type of bias can be controlled, providing some reliability for the coding process.[5]

Coding is thus a key component of the actual analysis of the data generated through organizational survey. By ensuring that the coding or scoring formats are uniformly applied and monitored, the survey administrator can increase the probability that the data to be analyzed are *not* biased but are as reliable and accurate as possible.

Data Analysis and Treatment

Once the data have been collected, edited, and coded, the information can now be put together in meaningful patterns for statistical analysis. However, prior to running the data through a number of statistical techniques, an analysis plan should be carefully formulated. Basically, such a plan establishes precisely what will be done with the data. As previously argued, data about the quality of work life in an organization should not be gathered simply because "it's out there." Rather, if the assessment is to have any real meaning for the organization, the plan of analysis should reflect earlier diagnoses of organizational problems and situations.

Meaningful data analysis requires two very basic types of "tools": conceptual tools and technical tools.[6] Good examples of conceptual tools for organizational analysis are the systems model and the notion of "fit" discussed in Chapters 1 and 2. Such conceptual models can specify the types of questions researchers should ask of the data. The diagnostic questions that are subsequently generated will help the surveyors to focus on key organizational issues. Technical tools reflect the range of statistical methods and techniques that enable the researcher to pose questions to a data set to ensure that the results will be reliable and not simply due to chance.

Since the first chapter of the text focuses on some of the conceptual tools necessary for a meaningful quality of work life assessment, this discussion will focus on the technical tools of data analysis. Remember, however, that the questions that are raised determine the outcome of the survey. Once the questions are decided, obtaining appropriate technical procedures for actually posing those questions to the data is relatively easy. Thus, the analysis of the data should be carefully planned during the earlier diagnosis and development stages of the survey process.

Since quality of work life surveys usually include both quantitative (closed-ended) and qualitative (open-ended) types of information, the plan of analysis must be adapted to the nature of the data being used. Because these two informational sources represent varied inputs in the survey process, it is important to distinguish between them for analytical purposes.

Quantitative Data Analysis

Statistical techniques appropriate for quality of work life assessment differ not only in the types of questions that the survey information attempts to answer but also in the *level of measurement* required of the information collected. For instance, if an organization is interested in knowing how satisfied people are with their jobs in general, then a simple tabulation of responses is all that is required. However, if the organization desires to follow up such general statements with questions of relative satisfaction from one job category as compared with another, or from one hierarchical level in the organization to another, then a slightly more sophisticated statistical technique, referred to as cross-tabulation, would be necessary. Finally, if the organization is interested in finding out the relative importance of a range of job-related demands on overall satisfaction, it is necessary to go beyond the univariate and bivariate types of analyses mentioned above. Thus, the statistical technique that will be the most appropriate for analysis depends on the nature of the question being asked of the data. However, since the appropriateness of statistical methods is also determined by the level of measurement represented in the data, a brief discussion of measurement issues is necessary before looking at the kinds of approaches available.

Levels of Measurement

As part of the data gathering and coding process, different values are assigned to the various answers given by the respondents. The practice of assigning these values constitutes the process of measurement. Since these values are differentiated from one another on the basis of the ordering and distance properties inherent in measurement rules, distinguishing between the levels of such measurement is important. For our present purposes, these different levels have been traditionally classified as nominal, ordinal, and interval types of data.[7]

Nominal level data constitute the lowest form of measurement. They come from categories where there is no single underlying continuum. Job classifications, for example, such as secretary, teller, or manager, would be considered nominal data. Although numerical values are often assigned to the different categories of response, they have no quantitative properties and only serve to identify the categorization. Since no assumption of ordering or distances between categories is made, any statistical technique that assumes such meaningful numerical distances between categories should not be used.

The next level of measurement, *ordinal level data*, does assume an underlying continuum. These data are rank-ordered according to a specific criterion; however, the amount of distance between the different categories involved is not known. For example, in quality of work life assessments employees are often asked to rate certain benefits they receive according to whether they are perceived to be "excellent," "good," "fair," or "poor." While it is thus possible to rank-order these perceptions in terms of relative value (for example, higher or lower), we do not know how much lower a response of "good" is compared to a feeling that the benefit involved is "excellent." Moreover, we cannot safely assume that the difference between "good" and "excellent," for example, is equal to the distance between "good" and "fair." The distances remain undefined.

The final level of measurement for our purposes is *interval*. Interval level data differ from ordinal data in that the distances between items or articles on an interval scale are known. Thus, in addition to ordering values, the distances between categories are defined in terms of fixed and equal units. The classic example of an interval level scale is a thermometer, which records temperatures in terms of degrees; one degree implies the same amount of heat whether the temperature is at the higher or lower end of the scale.

Although most behavioral science research data do not meet the rigorous standards of interval measurement, the data are often assumed to be close enough to interval standards that higher-order statistical methods are still employed. In the Likert-type scales discussed in Chapter 4, respondents are asked to rank-order their answers on a "strongly agree" to "strongly disagree" continuum. This type of measurement is clearly at the ordinal level. However, since the reliability of such scales tends to be quite good,[8] researchers often employ statistical techniques that assume interval data. This practice does violate basic statistical rules, but when ordinal scales *approach* interval standards, this procedure is often accepted. The approximation of such scales to interval level data, however, is only as good as the validity of the assumption. The important point to remember when selecting statistical methods is that statistics developed for one level of measurement can always be utilized with higher-level measures, but not with variables measured at a lower level.

Common Quantitative Data Analysis Techniques

A number of statistical techniques can be employed in quality of work life assessment. Since straight distributions and cross-tabulations of response are the most frequently used descriptive techniques, these will be briefly presented and illustrated in this section. For a fuller discussion of more sophisticated methods, the reader should consult the Appendix and some of the numerous sources on how to work with quantitative data.[9]

Frequency Distributions. Probably the most widespread and

simplest technique for describing survey data is the frequency distribution. Frequency distributions simply indicate the number and
percentage of respondents who answer in each of the available categories. These data, usually the first feedback a client will receive
from a particular attitude survey, give a broad overview of the feelings and opinions of members of an organization without getting into
specific pockets of discontent or extraordinary satisfaction.

Table 5–1 presents the frequency distribution for a series of job-
related questions from one of our recent surveys. As the figure
illustrates, this procedure readily shows the proportion of people
who respond favorably or unfavorably to a particular set of questions.
The distribution of response can be indicated in simple numbers or
in terms of percentage of response.

Cross-Tabulations. Frequency distributions provide information that describes the overall population of employee feelings. Just
as important, however, is considering possible differences among
groups of employees. For instance, in the example just given, we
know that 15 percent of the survey population "strongly agree" that
they are satisfied with their jobs, 48 percent "agree," and so forth.
But is this breakdown representative of all job classifications in the
organization? Are long-term employees more satisfied with their
jobs than those who have only worked for the organization for a short
period of time? Are those who report that they are *not* satisfied also
the ones who *do not* feel there is sufficient challenge in their jobs?

To find out where particular pockets of discontent or unique attitudes exist, the distributions of response must be cross-tabulated.
Thus, through a process of breaking down responses by a set of

Table 5–1   Frequency Distribution for Selected Survey Items

Question	Response (percent)				
	Strongly Agree	Agree	Neutral	Disagree	Strongly Disagree
Overall, I am satisfied with my job.	15	48	19	12	6
There is sufficient challenge in my job.	20	43	17	14	6
I feel I am adequately trained for my job.	20	60	12	6	2
My daily work hours are satisfactory.	23	58	6	8	6

Table 5–2　Example of a Cross-Tabulation for Job Satisfaction by Job Classification

Question: Overall, I am satisfied with my job.

Job Classification	Response (percent)				
	Strongly Agree	Agree	Neutral	Disagree	Strongly Disagree
Clerical	12	42	23	15	8
Secretarial	14	46	20	10	10
Teller	13	48	16	12	11
Head Teller	8	42	38	10	2
Professional Staff	18	55	9	16	2
Assistant Managers	22	69	4	5	0
Department Heads	20	63	17	0	0

subcategories determined by sociodemographic or other variables, researchers can be more explicit in describing the climate of an organization.

Table 5–2 takes the question on global job satisfaction initially presented in Table 5–1 and breaks it down by job classification. As these data indicate, levels of overall satisfaction generally increased with higher levels of organizational responsibility. However, head tellers were less satisfied than the other occupational groups. This type of analysis thus provides managers with a clearer indication of one job in relation to others in the organizations. It also points to specific areas in which further analysis is needed (for example, *why* are head tellers less satisfied; what does the large neutral response indicate; and so forth).

Beyond simple cross-tabulations, researchers may want to do slightly more complex aggregate data analysis. One way to isolate groups even more precisely is to control certain variables. Thus, if in Table 5–2 it were also desirable to control for sex or race, or possibly both at the same time, one could do a triple cross-tabulation to compare attitudes of males and females and minorities and non-minorities *within* similar job classifications.

There are essentially two times when researchers might want to control for a certain sociodemographic variable, such as sex, race, or educational level. One is when the sample (or population) is sufficiently large that various combinations of sociodemographic indices will provide more insight into organizational differences. The second instance is when there is a particular problem area and the researcher wants to isolate "problem" groups. At times, conducting a two- or three-way cross-tabulation to identify particular problems and groups within the organization is worthwhile.

One note of caution, however; although controlling for certain variables is often very helpful, researchers must be careful not to identify specific individuals. For example, assume that an organization employs 10 percent minorities out of an overall population of 250 persons. If the researchers simultaneously controlled for race and sex, they could certainly identify some of these individuals even in a relatively complex organization. By adding another control, such as length of employment, employees can be pinpointed even more precisely. Thus, if the researchers are not careful in reporting results to the client organization, they can destroy the confidentiality of participant response and the credibility of the survey.

This basic analytic technique is at the heart of quality of work life analyses. Because the procedure is not complicated, cross-tabulation can be understood by both respondents and managers of organizations. Thus groups of people who have uncharacteristic dissatisfaction or satisfaction on certain questions can be isolated, and specific response strategies that focus on those particular issues can be formulated. Moreover, both frequency distributions and cross-tabulations can be employed with *any* level of measurement.

In many instances organizations want to analyze their survey data more extensively; perhaps they wish to look at a range of supplemental questions concerning the job (for example, work hours, work load, challenge, responsibility, pay, advancement, and so on) and their *combined* effect on overall job satisfaction. When questions of this type are posed of the data, more intricate statistical techniques are required. Among these methods are correlations among variables, multiple regression, analysis of variance, and factor analysis. These techniques are discussed briefly in the Appendix. With the advent of computer technology and software statistical packages, of course, the use of these statistical procedures has grown rapidly over the past decade. Such advanced analysis techniques, however, must be used with care. The assumptions underlying each method must be clearly understood before any complex manipulation of the survey data is attempted. Furthermore, when assessing perceptions of the quality of work life in an organization, rather than focusing on such quantitative methods alone, written comments or interviews with respondents can lend further insight into explanations of employee attitudes and opinions.

Qualitative Data Analysis

Because qualitative analysis can provide additional in-depth insight into survey results, which cannot be obtained through quantitative data alone, qualitative data development should be considered in the early stages of the survey process. Following initial sensing sessions or pilot studies, open-ended, qualitative analysis is extremely beneficial. An analysis of preliminary open-ended data can raise questions for consideration, point to germane issues, and identify problem areas that can then be monitored more extensively through the creation of closed-ended survey questions. As delineated in Chapter 3, the comments and inputs of employees during these early phases often form the basis for many of the survey questions. At the very least, these data provide a check for appropriate questionnaire coverage.

In addition to the early gathering of qualitative data, the later inclusion of open-ended questions on the final survey can provide the organization with a good indication of the more intense feelings held by the employee population since the comments are often expressed in personal terms. Moreover, if specific problems do exist, these "free answer," open-ended questions provide respondents with an opportunity to tell the organization, in explicit terms, exactly where the problem lies. The difficulty with open-ended data, however, is in interpretation. Indeed, since the questions are "open-ended," the responses are also "open," spontaneous, and expressive. As briefly discussed in the earlier section on coding, organizational researchers must exercise care in the analysis and interpretation of these qualitative data.

In analyzing comments generated by questionnaires or interviews, essentially two basic approaches can be employed: *differential* and *integrative* analyses.[10] The first approach is a relatively straightforward form of content analysis, in which favorable and unfavorable comments about specific job- or organization-related concerns are categorized from each discrete comment. Differential analysis provides a basic indication of organizational strengths and weaknesses. Each of the open-ended questions is analyzed separately as the data analyst goes through each question and looks at all responses to that particular question before proceeding to the next question. As the analyst proceeds, a coding frame is developed for each question by creating a tally sheet on which different types of responses are categorized. When a response occurs that has been seen before, the analyst puts a tally mark in the appropriate box. Since those responses that occur frequently are likely to appear early in the analysis, one can usually look at the earlier-appearing categories and make a rough, but usually fairly accurate, estimate as to whether the response will be significant or not.

Integrative analysis is more subjective and requires greater expertise. In this approach open-ended comments are reviewed for common threads of meaning or association. Since comments that are focused on certain areas can also reflect more global themes, this type of analysis can orient managers to underlying concerns in their organization. For example, in a recent survey conducted in a research laboratory, a consistent theme that emerged from a number of open-ended questions was an underlying tension between the organization's administrative support personnel and the technical staff. The support personnel felt that the technical people did not value their contribution to the laboratory's goals, and as such this perception created a feeling of resentment and emerging dissatisfaction among the former group. These negative feelings alerted the laboratory's management to an important issue that had the potential of leading to increased friction in the work place.

Figure 5–1 presents a representative sample of open-ended comments taken from an attitude survey conducted in a medium-

Figure 5–1   A Random Sample of Comments Taken from an Attitude Survey in a Medium-Sized Savings Bank.

The One Thing Needed to Make This Bank a Better Place to Work Is . . .

Aside from the lack of space in my branch, our basic material needs are well taken care of. However, I would like to see more responsibility given to those who have proven that they can handle their present job duties. If more people could do other jobs within the bank, it would enable us to understand the importance of all areas in the bank. It would also better prepare those interested in moving up to a higher, more challenging position.

Better equipment to work with.

To adopt an attitude that it is the bank we are working for, and not only "my department," "my triad," or "my branch."

Get the various units in the bank working as one and not against each other.

We could use some sort of information concerning the different functions of other departments.

Fair distribution of work loads. If supervisors were to notice more often who is doing what and when it was done, it would greatly improve morale within the office.

More direct communication so that we know what is going on and are aware of why some policies are instituted.

More activities that involve group participation, such as the SBLI (Savings Bank Life Insurance) campaign.

More in-service training for all tellers.

The Things I Like Most About the Bank Are . . .

Co-workers are friendly and generally easy to work with.

The fact that we are a progressive bank; the people.

I believe that the bank shows a concern for its employees and they are a nice group to work with. The bank is also good about furthering education and it mostly promotes from within.

A steady income and the opportunity to run my branch as I please (within certain limitations).

Our benefits, hours, and working conditions.

Working in a department I enjoy; the exposure to many types of people and careers. On my own or through people in my own department, I am beginning to learn about the workings of the bank as a whole.

The people who work here and the fact that the bank as a whole is interested in helping people.

The Things I Like Least About the Bank Are . . .

Being transferred to other branches.

Management's refusal to recognize extra time put in by branch personnel on a daily basis without compensation. There is a lack of communication between branches and departments.

Cost of living raises are few and far between.

The low pay scale for a hard day's work.

The long hours which make commuting a problem both time and money wise.

Very often, there isn't enough help to do all the work.

Too many meetings.

The attitude of *some* of the supervisors. I find very little communication between tellers and managers. One has to hear about problems from the head teller that the supervisor is not happy with our work. Why can't the manager himself talk to tellers? Some managers act as if they are better than the tellers which upsets me greatly.

sized savings bank. Based on an initial reading of these responses, a coding scheme can be developed to summarize this information. For instance, from among the things that respondents report concerning what they like *most* about the bank, *differential analysis* would point to co-workers and organizational concern for employees as positive points in the bank's favor. By reading through the entire range of comments for all questions, *integrative analysis* would reveal a strong theme that the communication linkages between the bank's branches and its departments in the main office are weak. Since the communication theme runs through different questions, the organization can be more confident that it has located an important issue. Thus, while differential analysis is beneficial and enables the qualitative data to be condensed into tabular form, undertaking an integrative analysis will lend more support and specificity to organizational strengths and weaknesses.

One problem with integrative analysis, however, is that common themes or meanings are often not as apparent in the data and, in many instances, they are not there at all. In such cases, "themes" should not be created. One way to ensure that appropriate data are obtained and that the "reading" of the questionnaire comments is reflective of those responses is through the creation of an analysis outline. Essentially, the outline involves a six-step analytic process. [11]

1. *Specify needed data.* In developing a qualitative analysis outline, the surveyors must establish what data are required to delineate employee attitudes and expectations. For instance, if in preliminary diagnosis problems appear with specific organizational practices such as training programs, performance evaluation, or job posting systems, including open-ended questions concerning these issues may provide the organization with more information about the exact areas in which problems may exist. One approach is to give people who report dissatisfaction with a specific organizational policy the opportunity to state their dissatisfaction. Unless the focused open-ended questions on training are fully considered during preliminary diagnosis, the organization may simply find that there is a general dissatisfaction with training programs, but with no indication as to *why* that dissatisfaction exists.

2. *Create tabulation plans.* This step basically integrates coding analysis with the type of answer format used. For instance, on optical scanning response sheets open-ended questions are usually recorded on separate forms. If cross-tabulation analysis of the com-

ments is desired, the answer sheets must either be linked with a code number or include selected sociodemographic indicators on the top of the separate form. If open-ended questions are integrated on the answer sheet, linking the open-ended responses with the closed-ended responses is not necessary. When such code numbers are employed, however, the respondents must be informed of their use in keeping all responses from one person together and again reassured that their responses will be completely confidential.

3. *Create a tabulation scheme.* The next step is the creation of the codes. Coding can be accomplished by (1) preestablishing codes on the basis of organizational theory and/or preliminary diagnosis or (2) developing codes as the comments are read. In attempting to reflect accurately *what* is being said and *how* it is stated, an effective scheme can be based on a combination of these basic approaches. [12]

4. *Fill in categories for each variable.* As part of the tabulation scheme, a system of categories must be established for each variable. The system of categories for each question should be *exhaustive* (that is, a category in which to place each relevant item), and the categories should be *mutually exclusive* (that is, one and only one place to code an item within the system of categories). Thus each open-ended comment is unambiguously placed in a category. Comments which could be placed in one of a number of categories or which do not fit anywhere show that the category scheme is not mutually exclusive or exhaustive. Although appearing simple and obvious, this logical framework is frequently violated. Systems of categories that are organized around themes are especially prone to such errors.

5. *Establish procedures for categorization.* Specific working definitions of categorizations should be written down as part of the coding instructions. As mentioned earlier, these instructions should be as precise as possible and supported by examples to ensure an accurate reporting of the data.

6. *Pilot test the analysis outline.* Similar to the pilot testing of the survey prior to its actual implementation, trying out the qualitative analysis outline by different individuals not involved in the design of the survey and collection of the data can help uncover any needed modifications. If a number of coders are to be employed, this pilot testing is usually included as part of the training process. Even if a relatively small number of people are coding or if the surveyors themselves are coding the material, this stage should be included to control for potential personal bias (however subtle it may be) in what people may read into a set of comments.

As the procedures discussed in this section indicate, even for qualitative information some counting does take place. From the respondent's point of view, however, a quantitative type of question where an answer is simply checked off, circled, or marked is very different from an open-ended one. In a qualitative response the individual has an opportunity to put things in his or her own words, an important personalized component to the overall survey process and an effective method to obtain precise data on specific organizational strengths and weaknesses. If the analysis of the qualitative information is accomplished in a clear and concise manner, these data can provide the organization with a fuller picture of the nature of life within its sphere of influence.

Linkage Between Quantitative and Qualitative Analyses

One of the reasons organizations undertake quality of work life assessments is to diagnose potential and existing problems in the firm. A predicament that must be confronted, however, is that, at times, isolated problems can be exaggerated beyond their actual importance. For instance, the comments of a couple of people can *suggest* that the issue over which they have praises or complaints is representative of a wider range of employees when concern about the issue is, in fact, much more contained. As discussed in Chapter 2, one way to control for this possibility is to ensure that information is obtained from different sources through different data-gathering techniques. Once a researcher has obtained data from two or more sources, each of which confirms the other, the likelihood that the phenomenon in question is present is greatly increased.[13] If, for example, a scan of closed-ended questions suggests that benefits are well regarded, and the same finding appears in the open-ended responses, then researchers can confidently conclude that benefits are positively perceived in the organization. Similar independent confirmation can, and frequently does, occur for negative attitudes as well. By using the qualitative response, the actual meanings of the data can be more accurately reflected.

Another linkage between the two data sources is through a testing of the results found in one part of the survey by the other. In one of our surveys, content analysis of the open-ended responses pointed to a number of complaints about the role of the personnel department in performance appraisal and promotion decisions. In an attempt to analyze this perception more explicitly, a series of cross-tabulated analyses were undertaken by various sociodemographic indicators (for example, department, job classification, educational background, and so forth). In turn, related closed-ended questions were similarly analyzed. At first, no significant differences were found across job categories, departments, educational backgrounds, and so on. Continued analysis, however, revealed that respondents who reported that they did not know how the organization's performance evaluation system actually operated were disproportionately represented in the group who complained about personnel's role. Thus, rather than a system or specific group problem, the organization was faced with an informational problem. Intervention was subsequently focused on informing people what the actual role of personnel was in the evaluation process (that of an integrator rather than an actual decision-making body).

Clearly, having both qualitative and quantitative data on a survey is helpful. Each source of information makes the other source more complete. With quantitative data, comparisons can be made from year to year or across organizations. At the same time, the qualitative data give researchers an opportunity to look for trouble spots within the organization or problem issues such as relations with supervisors, cooperation between divisions, and the like. By obtaining and analyzing both types of data, the organization will have a more accurate delineation of specific issues and concerns.

Interpretation of Survey Results

After the data have been summarized, including both content and statistical analysis, the aggregate of information must be interpreted for its organizational meanings. This interpretation is accomplished through an assessment process in which the raw data are evaluated and the implications for the organization are drawn out. In many instances the interpretation of survey results is relatively straightforward and involves little more than reading the tables and using descriptive, qualitative data to help "explain" relationships between variables. At other times, when sample data or more complicated relationships are involved, interpretation can be quite an involved and intricate process. Most researchers depict such interpretation as both an art and a science.[14] It is an art in the sense that as an inherent part of the interpretive process, surveyors must exercise their own judgment and evaluation of what the data mean. It is a science in that a number of procedures can be followed and questions raised that add a tone of objectivity.

There are essentially two underlying problems in the interpretation of survey results: (1) attributing cause and effect relationships between variables on the basis of our assumptions and (2) establishing an appropriate base for evaluation.

One issue that must be considered carefully is *why* a particular organizational subunit responds to a set of questions in a given manner. A common difficulty in this type of interpretation occurs when people assume that they know the reason why something is being answered in a particular manner. One of the ways this is often done is by attributing some personality characteristic, usually unfavorable, to those who respond in a negative fashion. This tendency is referred to as *attribution*. As discussed in Chapter 1, attribution theory has gained widespread interest in psychological research in explaining how people interpret causality between different variables on the basis of assumptions they make about the situation. In one of our past surveys in a savings bank, for example, questions concerning interdepartmental communication and a reorganization to divisions elicited uniformly unfavorable responses. Some individuals in the organization interpreted this negative response as part of a general rigidity or resistance to organizational change. Based on this interpretation a solution was suggested: once people became more comfortable with the new organizational structure, the *perceived* communication problem would correct itself. Similar questions in subsequent years, however, reflected continued complaints about and criticisms of the lack of effective and timely interdepartmental communication. These subsequent findings strongly suggested that resistance to change was not a significant factor in the initial negative response, and that more extensive integrative mechanisms might be necessary to improve communication and coordination between departments. Thus, potential "solutions" and interventions can be quite different based on the attribution of the cause of the problem.

The important point is that interpretation of survey data is open to potential subjective distortion based on our assumptions. Thus, an organization's management should evaluate survey data at their face value, and *not* assume knowledge of *why* certain problems are reflected in the survey process. Rather, the data should be used to find out, in depth, why people feel and behave the way they do.

The second concern centers on the use of appropriate norms in evaluation of the data. The data presented in Table 5-1, for example, indicated that 63 percent of a bank's employee population either "strongly agreed" or "agreed" that they perceived an overall sense of satisfaction with their present job. How should the meaning of this finding be interpreted? Does this represent a strong feeling of job satisfaction? Or should the surveyor report that 18 percent disagreed that they felt an overall sense of such satisfaction? In many instances, of course, there are logical extremes of universal dissatisfaction versus universal satisfaction. In this instance, however, the analyst faces an intermediate statistic that could be appraised in a number of different ways. This example illustrates the fact that survey results must be interpreted in a relative manner. Thus industry norms or past survey results on the same organization may prove beneficial to a more complete understanding of the present data.

Descriptive Surveys

Surveys can be developed without using existing norms or standards. This type of quality of work life assessment can provide the organization with descriptive information about the ways in which employees perceive various aspects of the job and their overall working environment. Descriptive surveys are often used to generate organizational norms that can be used for comparative purposes in subsequent surveys. Even during the initial data-gathering process, of course, the information can provide management with some guidelines as to the nature of organizational strengths and weaknesses.

In descriptive surveys different groups throughout the organization are usually examined in relation to each other. This technique provides the opportunity to use subgroup norms as a basis for interpretation of relative satisfaction or dissatisfaction from one job category to another, one department to another, or any subunit to the organization as a whole. The comparative nature of a descriptive survey thus allows a management team to obtain insight into differences across various groups in their organization. The procedure, however, has some basic weaknesses.

In a recent bank survey tellers had a significantly lower level of job satisfaction than the other job clusters. Since tellers in all banks typically express less job satisfaction and more frustration than other bank-related occupational groups, this finding is not as significant as knowing how these tellers compare to tellers in other banking organizations, or how their attitudes compare to those held in previous years. Moreover, a comparison based on subgroup norms alone can produce misleading findings. That branch managers might be more satisfied than tellers and secretaries, for instance, could lead to a false reassurance of managerial satisfaction if these branch managers were actually less satisfied than they were one or two years earlier, or if they were less satisfied relative to branch managers in different banking organizations.

Comparison of Survey Results over Time

A major advantage of an ongoing survey-based quality of work life assessment program is that the findings from one year can be compared with and contrasted to survey results obtained during subsequent periods. If data have been gathered over a relatively long period of time, trends in attitudes and reactions to specific organizational programs and policies can be monitored, thus providing a fuller basis for interpreting the meaning of the data.

These results must still, however, be interpreted with caution. Since small changes or shifts in attitudes usually reflect chance variations over time, they should not be interpreted as significant change. Moreover, even the interpretation of the reasons underlying major differences or shifts in attitudes from one time period to another must be done with care since the change might be attributable to other intervening factors.

As an illustration of this pitfall, we can look to a survey that points to a specific organizational problem. Once the organization's management decides to address the issue, positive outcomes are usually expected by the employee population. Although re-surveys often show that such intervention has led to at least some improvement, at other times follow-up surveys will suggest that the various steps taken have not significantly alleviated the initial problem. Management must then reassess what has already been done and what new interventions might be necessary.

In one of our bank surveys the effectiveness of the organization's training programs emerged as a problem. Based on this information, the firm's president and the vice president of human resources decided to create a new position for someone to direct and oversee its training programs. The new training director was appointed from within the bank—an individual who had a background in human resource management, including training, and who was generally well liked by his peers and superiors. Subsequently, the training director updated existing programs and created new ones. Expectations were high that the next survey would favorably reflect the new training director's efforts. The result, however, was deep disappointment. Not only did scores reflecting attitudes about training programs decline, but they declined dramatically. At the same time, there was a sense that the training director had been quite effective in rejuvenating current programs and formulating new ones and that people felt better qualified in their *own* jobs. These apparently conflicting findings puzzled the bank's management.

Some concepts emerging from research concerning types of change after organization development interventions can shed some light on what happened.[15] Basically, three levels of change can occur after such interventions: *alpha, beta*, and *gamma*. *Alpha change* is a positive change on the same scale that was used to identify the problem. Thus, if on the follow-up survey question, "The training programs at the bank are effective," the mean response goes from disagree to agree, everyone would conclude that some important, positive changes had taken place. If, however, people felt that the training director had been effective and had made some important changes, but the mean score on the training-effectiveness question either remained unfavorable or went from disagree to strongly disagree, people would seriously question whether the training director had, in fact, done a good job. Often when people think that something has been a problem and someone is assigned the responsibility to correct it, increased attention is focused on that issue. This can lead to a "recalibration" of the measuring scale as it is applied to that issue. Thus, even though the interventions might have produced more effective training programs, because of the heightened awareness and sensitivity to the training issue, employees might be more critical than they were in the initial survey. This attitude is referred to as *beta change*, where anecdotal or performance data indicate that improvement has, in fact, occurred, but is not reflected as an improvement on the original scale. A decrease in job-related errors or concerns dealt with through training, along with an increased questioning about training effectiveness, would be an example of a beta change.

Finally, *gamma change* refers to the situation in which the original scale is no longer meaningful. In many instances the importance of issues does change over time. For example, the fact that coordination between tellers and customer service personnel is now perceived to be a more important issue than training effectiveness would suggest a shift of meaningfulness from the issue of training to coordination among different job clusters. This type of *gamma change* can subsequently influence how people respond to a particular set of questions.

Thus, even when comparing survey results from one period to another, trends in employee opinions and attitudes must be carefully analyzed. Through the use of qualitative information, the probing of causal relationships, and the examination of specific survey questions in the context of related organizational information and phenomena (for example, related questions, performance data, and so forth), a meaningful basis for interpreting the actual meaning of the survey results can be established. By assessing the data in this relative context, the organization can develop a greater understanding of its climate over time.

Industry Norms

Another useful context in which to interpret data from quality of work life assessments is through the use of industry norms. Since many consulting firms specialize in organizational surveys, they often use standardized questionnaires with associated local, industry, or national norms. These norms can present the organization with a clearer indication of how its employees, either at the organizational or subunit level, compare attitudinally to similar groups in other firms.

The main problem with this type of analysis is essentially twofold. First, since such surveys are standardized, the questions are fairly general in nature and might not reflect specific organizational issues. Second, in a relatively turbulent environment, data that have been collected as recently as six months to one year earlier in other organizations might not be truly comparative. In fact, by virtue of changes that have occurred in the environment surrounding an organization, a particular firm might appear to be either in a more favorable or more unfavorable position relative to other firms, depending on factors that are beyond its influence. Thus, judgment is required in this interpretive process as well.

Both industry norms and past institutional findings can be useful for an organization in its attempt to assess employee attitudes. Perhaps the most useful information is recent institutional findings on which management has instituted some changes. Subsequent follow-up efforts to evaluate changes and reassess attitudes can provide the most accurate picture of the nature of work life in a particular organization. These might consist of either sensing or polling sessions, or even "mini-surveys."

Feedback of Survey Results

Survey results can be reported to organizational members through either written or verbal reports. While both types of reporting techniques are useful, a combination of the two is usually the most productive. Moreover, this process tends to be most effective when *all* participants receive some form of feedback. Since each group within the organization involved in the survey process will usually have an interest in its results, all organizational levels, from top management to lower-level employees, should receive some written or verbal information concerning the results of the survey.

In surveys we have done, a brief, general written report to all participants has always been used. Included in the report are the major findings, both favorable and unfavorable, and a summary of the distributions—the percentages in the strongly agree to strongly disagree continuum—for the closed-ended questions. In addition to this general report, an in-depth discussion of the survey results is given to the organization's management team and the personnel office. This report contains detailed information (cross-tabulations, relationships between the major subsections of the survey, summaries of the sensing group sessions, and so forth) from the survey process. It adds a valuable dimension for managers and enables them to identify particular areas within the organization that might require more attention than others.

In addition to the written materials provided for the various sectors of an organization, having some general discussions of the results is also helpful. In one of the organizations we have surveyed, the results have been customarily reviewed with the president and the personnel officers. In another, general meetings with representatives of the groups covered by the survey were held. Such sessions provide an opportunity for the survey consultants to clarify possible ambiguities in the data and to discuss any questions that might arise. While these meetings can be held at any time during the feedback process, at least one meeting should be held prior to the submission of the "final" report. This session can prepare and inform organizational members for the more formal report to come. Subsequent meetings can then be held to further clarify and discuss the results.

Nature of the Feedback

The results generated from a quality of work life survey can provide an organization with a "mirror" of the perceptions and attitudes of its work force. For this feedback to be effective, however, organizational members must perceive it as valid, reliable, and pertinent to the organization. Thus, as part of the reporting process, it is important to consider some of the following characteristics of effective feedback.[16]

- *Timeliness.* For the results of the survey to be useful to the organization, the information should be fed back as quickly as possible. Once more than a couple of months have elapsed between the administration of the survey and the reporting of the results, the effectiveness of the survey process will be significantly reduced.
- *Relevance.* The information reported to managers and survey participants should be relevant to the important issues that emerged in the survey. By focusing on peripheral issues, an organization will only diminish the credibility of the survey process.
- *Clarity.* Feedback should be straightforward and easily understood. The language, symbols, and form used in reporting the results should be both familiar and understandable to the target audience.
- *Descriptiveness.* If feedback is to be useful to the organization, it should describe actual conditions and perceptions in the firm. It should be specific and detailed, but also unbiased; it is important to avoid an evaluative tone. The reports (either written or verbal) should contain the attitudes of the employee population (or subpopulations) and *not* an evaluation of those feelings. This decreases the probability that participants will feel threatened by the results.

- *Comparativeness.* As discussed in the interpretation section, survey data are often ambiguous and should be analyzed within a set context. This should be made clear in the reporting of the results (for example, descriptive surveys comparing subgroups within the organization, comparisons over time, industry norms).
- *Openness.* Quality of work life assessments are not panaceas to organizational problems. Rather, such efforts can only serve to identify *some* major concerns and point to areas that require attention. Thus, the feedback should not be used as an end in itself. For the survey process to be truly effective, the formal reporting of the data should be viewed as a starting point for in-depth discussion and problem solving. To encourage this openness, any data reports should reflect this process.

Report Presentation

An important part of feeding back survey results to employees and managers is presentation of the data, which should be done as clearly and as briefly as possible. A potential problem that often emerges from organizational surveys is data overload. So much information —computer printout on top of computer printout—is given to people that they simply become overwhelmed. This reduces rather than reinforces the importance of the survey process.

The initial report to the participants should thus be limited to the major areas of concern that emerge from the survey. While all individuals should be provided with a general overview of the survey results for the overall organization, detailed information given to specific groups should reflect only those data that are relevant to their particular needs. In surveys we have conducted, these participant reports usually include five basic sections:

1. A *brief introduction*, which describes the survey process, how the questionnaire was formulated, how the data were gathered, and who participated (sociodemographic description).
2. An *overview* of the results, which highlights the areas that received particularly high *and* particularly low favorability ratings, and briefly delineates the content or theme(s) obtained from open-ended questions.
3. A brief discussion of attitudes toward the *major subsections* of

the survey (e.g., attitudes toward pay, management, job security, job satisfaction, etc.).

4. *Concluding comments* summarizing changes from earlier surveys, comparisons with other organizations, and/or placing the findings in their environmental context. This also includes a call for discussion and probing of the survey results.

5. *Distributional data* for the closed-ended questions, which indicate the proportion of employees who responded from "strongly agree" to "strongly disagree" for the different items. These are presented in tabular form at the end of the report.

As indicated earlier, reports to middle and upper-level management are more extensive. While the initial parts are similar to those discussed above (for example, brief introduction and general overview of the findings), management reports then proceed with detailed descriptions of the major subsections of the survey by job classification, department, and other functional and sociodemographic items of interest. In our experience, reports are usually subdivided by issues, with the entire discussion of a particular issue (for example, pay and benefits) delineated completely before moving on to the next issue. These discussions are combined with tabular or graphic displays of the data (usually favorability versus unfavorability). When combined with verbal discussions and meetings that focus on the meanings of these data for the organization, this process can ensure that the feedback that emerges from the survey will provide the organization with a sound basis to assess, and ultimately improve, the quality of working life within its boundaries.

Organizational Follow-Up: The Utilization of Survey Results

So far, the entire survey process has simply indicated to the organization various areas and issues within its parameters that are viewed favorably, unfavorably, or with a mixed reaction. The onus is now on management to utilize this information to deal with important organizational concerns. Although a firm's management can use this information in a number of ways, and although there is no "one best way" to implement the follow-up process, certain issues should be considered.

A growing body of literature is pointing to the effectiveness of survey feedback as a way of establishing a context for organizational improvement.[17] An important theme underlying these discussions is employee involvement in the evaluation and planning of proposed "solutions" to problems identified in such surveys. By involving employees in all phases of the survey process, resistance to the results ("They were all misleading questions anyway"), rationalization for negative findings ("The people in my department always complain; it's their nature"), and resistance to proposed courses of action ("This is just another meaningless policy change") can be minimized.

One established way of generating reaction to the survey results and maintaining involvement is the use of employee follow-up groups. In one of the organizations in which we have conducted an ongoing survey feedback program, the management team decided to assemble a follow-up group composed of individuals from a number of different departments and functional areas throughout the firm. As in the use of sensing groups, this "diagonal slice" was composed of employees who did *not* have any reporting relationships with each other. These individuals met on a weekly basis to discuss the results of the survey and to propose courses of action for the organization. Throughout these meetings the consultants served as a resource base, providing more information and in-depth analysis of the data, which focused on specific problems and issues being examined by the group.

One potential problem with this approach is "survey overkill"—a tendency for discussion and analysis of the data to become so prolonged that the effectiveness of any action is greatly diminished. The first time the organization tried this technique the follow-up group met for one year with a final report due at the end of that period. When solutions were finally proposed, the issues underlying the solutions were no longer in the forefront of organizational concern, and many individuals denied that the problems still existed. During the next survey intervention, the follow-up group was given a three-month time frame in which to formulate its recommendations. The group's concerns were still on people's minds at the end of the shorter time period, and solutions to the problems were more fully acknowledged by management and the rest of the organization. Clearly, timetables should be established to clarify goal expectations and set deadlines for the follow-up group's reports and recommendations.

A second approach is the use of external consultants. In another organizational survey feedback effort, the results indicated some negative perceptions about the personnel department. These centered around the salary classification system, the department's role in performance appraisal and promotions, and the feeling that the personnel department did *not* concern itself with the employees' best interests. Instead of using an employee-based follow-up group, the organization retained a consultant who assisted in establishing a new salary classification system, in informing the work force more fully about personnel's role, and in helping the personnel department reorganize, based on the feedback from the survey.

In other instances, when the issues involved are relatively simple, an organization's management can deal with them successfully through their own intervention. Indeed, since issues that emerge from organizational surveys are often related to specific dissatisfactions with working conditions, out-dated equipment, and other contextual factors, these complaints can be readily rectified through relatively simple management decisions. The important consideration in these instances is to inform the employee population that these changes are being made based on the feedback from the organizational survey.

In summary, there is no "one correct way" to implement the follow-up process after an attitude survey. Whether an organization should use employee follow-up groups, outside consultants, or in-house managers to handle the results of the survey depends on the complexity of the problems and the organization's capability and comfort in solving these problems. Regardless of the approach selected, however, the organization must treat these issues in a forth-right manner. The organizational "grapevine" is usually quite sensitive to these concerns, and if there are any perceptions that certain issues are being ignored or bypassed, the survey process and problem-solving procedure that follows will lose all credibility. In the long term, this can create more harm than good for the organization in question.

Ongoing Survey Feedback Efforts

The approach that we have described in this book is part of an ongoing process of diagnosing organizational strengths and weaknesses, obtaining information about employee attitudes and perceptions, analyzing those data for their relevance to the organization, and then using those data as a basis for organizational improvement and development. This is not a one-time procedure. The process, to be most effective, should be part of a continual quality of work life program. In our efforts, we have done this on a two-year cycle.

Although every two years may seem like a lot of time and effort to expend monitoring employee attitudes and perceptions of the work place, the communication that results can provide managers with a fuller understanding of changes in the organization's climate. By providing employees at all levels the opportunity to participate in this process—shaping ideas for questions, receiving the results, and actual problem solving—effective upward and downward communication channels can be established. By examining the information generated from subsequent surveys, managers can also learn a great deal about change processes and their own development. Considering the rapid changes we are currently experiencing in our business environment, this ongoing effort to create meaningful communication and interaction with all levels of an organization will be an increasingly important component of human resource management.

Endnotes

1. R.B. Dunham and F.J. Smith, *Organizational Surveys: An Internal Assessment of Organizational Health* (Glenview, Ill.: Scott, Foresman, 1979); C. Moser and G. Kalton, *Survey Methods in Social Investigation* (New York: Basic Books, 1974); A.N. Oppenheim, *Questionnaire Design and Attitude Measurement* (New York: Basic Books, 1966).
2. C. Moser and G. Kalton, *ibid.*, pp. 410–14.
3. R.B. Dunham and F.J. Smith, *op. cit.*, p. 92.
4. For a more complete discussion of content analysis, see C. Moser and G. Kalton, *op. cit.*, pp. 414–28; C. Selltiz, M. Jahoda, M. Deutsch, and S.W. Cook, *Research Methods in Social Relations* (New York: Holt, Rinehart & Winston, 1959); O.R. Holsti, *Content Analysis for the Social Sciences and Humanities* (Reading, Mass.: Addison-Wesley, 1969); G. Lindzey and E. Aronson (eds.), *The Handbook of Social Psychology, Vol. 2: Research Methods* (Reading, Mass.: Addison-Wesley, 1968).
5. A.N. Oppenheim, *op. cit.*, pp. 227–40.
6. D. Nadler, *Feedback and Organization Development: Using Data-Based Methods* (Reading, Mass.: Addison-Wesley, 1977), pp. 141–43.
7. These levels of measurement were first developed by S.S. Stevens, "On the Theory of Scales of Measurement," *Science 103* (1946), pp. 677–80. A discussion of their properties and importance can be found in most statistics and methodology texts for the social sciences. See, for example, N.H. Nie, C.H.

Hull, J.G. Jenkins, K. Steinbrenner, and D. Bent, *SPSS: Statistical Package for the Social Sciences* (New York: McGraw-Hill, 1975), Chapter 1; R.P. Runyon and A. Haber, *Fundamentals of Behavioral Statistics* (Reading, Mass.: Addison-Wesley, 1972), Chapter 3.

8. A.N. Oppenheim, *op. cit.*, pp. 140–41; R.P. Runyon and A. Haber, *ibid.*, p. 16.

9. Among the many books on quantitative analysis are N.H. Nie, *et al.*, *op. cit.*; W.L. Hays, *Statistics* (New York: Holt, Rinehart & Winston), 1963; J.T. Roscoe, *Fundamental Research Statistics for the Behavioral Sciences* (New York: Holt, Rinehart & Winston, 1969); R.P. Runyon and A. Haber, *op. cit.*

10. R.B. Dunham and F.J. Smith, *op. cit.*, pp. 96–100.

11. This discussion draws heavily on D.P. Cartwright's chapter, "Analysis of Qualitative Material," in L. Festinger and D. Katz (eds.), *Research Methods in the Behavioral Sciences* (New York: Dryden Press, 1953), pp. 421–70.

12. For a complete discussion of these concerns, see B. Berelson, *Content Analysis in Communication Research* (Glencoe, Ill.: The Free Press, 1952).

13. E.J. Webb, D.T. Campbell, R.D. Schwartz, and B. Sechrest, *Unobtrusive Measures: Nonreactive Research in the Social Sciences* (Chicago: Rand-McNally, 1966), p. 3; A.J. Vidich and G. Shapiro, "A Comparison of Participant Observation and Survey Data," in N.K. Denizen (ed.), *Sociological Methods: A Sourcebook* (New York: Aldine-Atherton, 1970), pp. 512–24.

14. The subjective and objective nature of survey interpretation are discussed in R.B. Dunham and F.J. Smith, *op. cit.*, pp. 101–03; C. Moser and G. Kalton, *op. cit.*, pp. 466–67; H. Hyman, *Survey Design and Analysis: Principles, Cases and Procedures* (New York: The Free Press, 1955), pp. 126–37.

15. R. Golembiewski, K. Billingsley and S. Yeager, "Measuring Change by OD Designs," *Journal of Applied Behavioral Science* 12:2 (April/May/June, 1976), pp. 133–57.

16. For a complete discussion of the nature of the feedback process in organizations, see Nadler, *op. cit.*, Chapter 8; P.L. Quaglieri, "Feedback: Is It All Useful?" *Leadership and Organization Development Journal* 1:4 (1980), pp. 13–15; J. Annett, *Feedback and Human Behavior* (Baltimore: Penguin Books, 1969); T. Rickards and J. Bessant, "A Mirror for Change: Survey/Feedback Experiences," *Leadership and Organization Development Journal* 1:2 (1980), pp. 10–14.

17. M.R. Cooper, B.S. Morgan, P.M. Foley, and L.B. Kaplan, "Changing Employee Values: Deepening Discontent?" *Harvard Business Review* 57:1 (1979), pp. 117–25; D. Sirota and A.D. Wolfson, "Pragmatic Approach to People Problems," *Harvard Business Review* 51:1 (1973), pp. 120–28; D.G. Bowers, "O.D. Techniques and Their Results in 23 Organizations," *Journal of Applied Behavioral Science* 9:1 (1973); D. Nadler, "Use of Feedback for Organizational Change," *Group and Organizational Studies* 1:1 (1976); S. Gellerman, *Behavioral Science in Management* (Baltimore: Penguin Books, 1974), Chapter 3.

Chapter 6

ORGANIZATIONAL SURVEYS: THEIR POTENTIAL, LIMITATIONS, AND PITFALLS

As one of the principal methodologies in organizational development efforts, survey feedback programs have gained increased prominence in contemporary business organizations. The model proposed here outlines the many issues that should be considered for an effective survey feedback program. This approach, however, is not a panacea for all organizational problems. Indeed, the main outcome from this process is the development of a foundation upon which an organization can improve the quality of its working life. As such, survey feedback is not an end but a *beginning* for meaningful organizational intervention and development.

Problems still exist, however, and are frequently beyond an organization's control. While internal efforts to probe the quality of work life can provide a basis for dealing with organizational problems in an anticipatory, proactive manner, the external environment can exert a significant influence on employee perceptions and attitudes. Many organizations have difficulty adapting to rapidly changing, turbulent environments. Considering the open-system nature of organizations, these external influences can pose limitations on the effectiveness of internal policies and interventions. Thus, the environmental context in which an organization operates must also be considered when discussing quality of work life issues.

Finally, a cautionary note must be mentioned. By simply conducting a quality of work life survey, an organization is unlikely to develop increased job satisfaction and organizational commitment on the part of its employee population. If the process becomes a matter of simply administering survey after survey, with little or no real effort for change, the outcome is likely to be increased apathy, indifference, or even resentment instead of a stronger commitment to the job and the organization. Managers must be aware that organizational diagnosis and data collection are only the first stage of the process proposed here; meaningful feedback and focused intervention constitute essential components for managerial purposes.

This final chapter looks at these concerns as a way of developing a firmer basis for not only assessing the quality of working life in contemporary organizations but also for improving it.

Survey-Based Organization Development Efforts

As just mentioned, survey feedback should not be viewed as an end in itself. The process of surveying employee attitudes and opinions and feeding back that information to those individuals is a practical organization development tool to diagnose existing problems, identify potential conflicts, and formulate a forum for two-way communication and discussion.

Organization development (OD) is usually defined as "the application of behavioral science knowledge in a long-range effort to improve an organization's ability to cope with changes in its external environment and increase its internal problem-solving capabilities."[1] Since OD .takes a systemic, long-range view of such change, its overall success depends heavily on proper diagnosis and evaluation, and the selection of appropriate intervention strategies. The approach discussed in this book presents a systemswide orientation to such development. It is particularly useful for assessing the need for organizational restructuring efforts, the effectiveness of organizational policies and procedures, satisfaction with the way in which jobs are designed, and the effectiveness of training programs, among other organizational concerns. As a basis for illustrating how attitudinal survey data can be used, some of these interventions will be discussed briefly in the following pages.

Organizational Restructure

Behavioral science research strongly suggests that organizations with many hierarchical levels (centralization) are more effective in rela-lively stable environments, while organizations with few hierarchical levels (decentralization) are more effective in turbulent environments. Unfortunately, since there is no common agreement on an environmental turbulence scale, defining just when an environment actually becomes "turbulent" is often difficult. Moreover, such turbulence has usually been defined in market and/or technological terms. The fact that the economy, social values, or the laws may also be changing has usually not been considered in assessing environmental stability or turbulence. A bank, for instance, might appear to be in a relatively stable environment. However, when one considers the changes brought about by the money markets, the limitations on interest allowed by thrift institutions, changing interest rates, and the general realignment of where people place their money, the environment can hardly be called stable.

While the fit between the actual level of environmental turbulence and appropriate organizational structure is difficult to delineate in practice, a survey feedback program can enable an organization to assess the effectiveness of its present structure. If the data indicate that poor coordination and communication exist between departments and/or branches, then organizational restructure might be a possibility. Depending on the extent of the communication/coordination "problem," this restructure could involve the use of cross-functional groups or simply the combination of one department's duties with those of another. If the problem is more extensive, entire levels of an organization may have to be eliminated and the decision-making process relegated to a lower level. This type of change is frequently made in organizations in which the technical expertise lies with employees at lower levels of the organization rather than with managers (for example, high-technology R&D firms). By using the data generated by a survey as a basis for further intervention and decisions, an organization can move toward a more effective fit with its environment.

Assessment of Training Needs

Traditional books and articles on industrial training suggest three phases or levels of assessing training needs: organizational, job, and person analyses. Organizational analysis examines the goals, objectives, and overall training needs of the organization. These activities are frequently performed by a long-range planning committee or by corporate executives who determine the macro-orientation of the organization. Job analysis focuses on specific training requirements, wage and salary administration issues, personnel selection, and promotion and transfer procedures. Although there is a good deal in common between a job analysis done for wage and salary administration and one conducted for training purposes, these analyses do vary in complexity based on the number of functions involved. The job description that emerges from this type of analysis, however, can enumerate the particular training needs of a given position. Finally, person analysis is a detailed performance appraisal of one incumbent on the job. Since this analysis outlines the particular strengths and weaknesses that a particular individual displays on the job, training programs tailored to individual needs can subsequently be created.

Survey research usually will uncover training needs for a category of people or a type of job, rather than individual needs. Thus, survey-based approaches are more effective for organization and job-level analyses than for person analysis. When combined with interviews and in-depth discussions with organizational members, however, this approach can readily point to both general and specific training needs and/or problems (see Chapter 2).

Job Redesign

As discussed in Chapter 1, the terms "blue-collar blues" and "white-collar woes" have come into frequent use. While the issue of worker discontent in contemporary America remains controversial, many social observers argue that dissatisfaction has emerged from the routinization of work and a scientific management mentality in the design of jobs. To confront what appears to be a steady decline in work-related satisfaction,[2] many jobs have been restructured so that employees will take more of an interest in their work and subsequently perform better.[3]

Three basic possibilities exist for job redesign: job rotation, job enlargement, and job enrichment. *Job rotation* is simply having people do different jobs on a regular basis. The rationale behind job rotation is that variety will improve morale, and output will be higher than in jobs without skill variety. Its use was popular in the late 1940s and early 1950s, particularly in the automobile industry. Although job rotation was the first step in job redesign, skill variety alone does not usually have the intended effect of increasing worker satisfaction and performance.

Similar to job rotation, *job enlargement* adds activities that are on the same level. A relatively simple, repetitive job, for example, can be enlarged by adding other tasks that augment the original job. These tasks may or may not have anything to do with each other, and, like job rotation, the idea is to provide some variety in the incumbent's work day. While used with some success, job rotation and enlargement are not perceived as an organization development effort by most practitioners since they really do not add anything meaningful to the job.[4]

Job enrichment, sometimes referred to as vertical job enlargement, is a procedure whereby a job is redesigned to include activities that would have come before (planning) and after (evaluation) the original job. This can provide a sense of job closure, in which the worker has more of an understanding of the entire work process. For instance, in a medical monitor manufacturing plant workers used to just bolt a few pieces together before the equipment drifted down the assembly line. The workers did not have any sense of how the entire job fit together or how the machine really operated. Moreover, as might be expected, the jobs on the assembly line were very dull. After jobs were "enriched," the work included not only manufacturing the entire medical monitor, but arranging for parts beforehand and checking the instrument after it was assembled. The assembly line was eliminated, and employees worked in small groups. Subsequently, the work force was more satisfied, and the quality of the machines was higher. The rate of production was about the same as before, but since the quality was higher, the cost of goods sold was lower.[5]

Survey research can help identify jobs that are candidates for enrichment.[6] By assessing response patterns for job-related questions on an attitude survey, managers can isolate jobs that are problematic. Clearly, some jobs are hard to make more challenging. Moreover, in many instances the cost and effort required may not be possible. Still, survey research can identify "problem" jobs so that if job enrichment is a possibility, the redesign effort can be more effectively focused and implemented.

The External Environment

In spite of internal efforts to improve the quality of work life in an organization, the external environment may actually exert a more significant influence on employee opinions than any organization development intervention. Indeed, there may be changes in responses from one survey to another which have little to do with what has gone on inside the organization. Rather, these perceptions may be due to events occurring outside the organization. Research suggests that the organization's environment is the most potent dimension regarding organizational change.[7] That is, nothing an organization does to improve functioning, such as redesigning jobs, restructuring, establishing training programs, and so forth, has as much effect on the organization's operations as does the environment. Therefore, survey feedback efforts have to be considered within the broader context of organizational-environmental strategies.

One of the most common responses to the environment is an attempt to control it. However, even extremely large organizations may fail in their attempts to do so. Witness the lack of success the automobile industry experienced in stemming the tide of foreign competition in the late 1970s and early 1980s.

Thompson, in a tightly reasoned book, noted five ways that organizations try to "control" their environments.[8] First, "under norms of rationality," organizations try to isolate their core technologies from these external influences. In other words, organizations maintain input and output mechanisms to keep the core task of the organization operating smoothly. In manufacturing organizations, for instance, purchasing and parts inventories are input mechanisms, and marketing is an output mechanism. Although not used much anymore, banks have maintained a provision that says the firm can control when people can withdraw funds from a regular passbook account (output) as well as offer "term" accounts that attempt to provide some control in the system. These mechanisms thus deal with the environment by attempting to reduce the influence of outside forces on internal operations. If these attempts to isolate the core tasks fail, organizations will often move toward more formalized input and output approaches. These formal components are what Thompson regards as a second stage of development.

Third, if the formal structures do not work very well, the organization can attempt to "smooth out" its input and output transactions. Ordinarily, managers will place more emphasis on one or the other side of the organization. Automobile companies often have sales contests and engage in price cutting to keep the manufacturing process operating at an efficient level (output). If there is an oversupply of a particular model on hand, automobile companies often reduce the number of component parts ordered from suppliers and slow production (input). In any event, there is an attempt to keep the core technology going at an even, predictable rate.

The fourth stage occurs if these buffering and leveling approaches do not work. In other words, if the smoothing procedures are not effective and the core technologies are being affected by external forces, the organization must better anticipate and adapt to environmental changes. To continue with the example of the automobile industry, it is well known that sales tend to increase following the introduction of a new model (usually in the early fall). Sales then tend to decline until early spring. If an automobile company can adjust its production to known periods of high and low demand, it will not have parking lots filled with unsold cars. Thus anticipation and prediction are important planning devices for most organizations.

Even prediction and anticipation, however, do not always work, and so one final stage may be necessary—rationing. Consumers see this as "one item per buyer." Automobile dealers may be able to get only one car per month in a very popular model line. Finally, the post office may place first-class mail in a top priority and attend to junk mail when there are lulls in postal traffic.

The point underlying the foregoing discussion is that, rather than try to isolate itself from the environment, an organization should position itself to adapt quickly to environmental change. An attitude survey can provide information useful in determining the best way for an organization to respond to its environment. Although such survey data are obviously limited in their effect on the environment, they can help an organization understand its environment better. For instance, if inflation has been rapid and wages and salaries have not kept pace, one probably does not need to know the results of an attitude survey to surmise accurately that there will be some dissatisfaction with pay. Still, there may be a differential of dissatisfaction between salary grades. People at higher salary grades may be more or less dissatisfied than people at lower grades. Survey data can thus provide managers with important information in their attempts to confront such issues.

Ultimately, the environment has the most dramatic effects on an organization. A particular company may have a proactive, anticipatory approach to management issues and development procedures. Jobs may be enriched, the structure may be appropriate for the environment, and the internal climate may be functional for the organization and its members. But if the external environment is turbulent due to economic, social, legal, or technological change, these dimensions can influence employee attitudes within the organization to a potentially more significant degree than internal policies or procedures. Thus, emphasis should be placed on the use of *appropriate* norms for interpretive purposes. Moreover, these data should be considered in their *appropriate* environmental context. Then, managers will have more insight into both how the environment is affecting their organization and how organizational members *perceive* this impact.

"What, Another Attitude Survey?"

Traditionally, employee opinion and attitude surveys have essentially been viewed as information-gathering tools solely for management's use. Even within this narrow orientation, however, the fact is that most managers have failed to utilize survey research to improve organizational performance.[9] Indeed, there is an important distinction between simply authorizing a survey and applying the results to organizational concerns. When employees take the time and effort to complete an attitude survey, expectations will rise that the information generated will be *used* to improve facets of the quality of work life in the organization. If the survey results are ignored by management, participants can subsequently experience an increased sense of frustration. Moreover, as mentioned at the beginning of this chapter, the outcome of this frustration often leads to dysfunctional job-related behaviors such as apathy, turnover, absenteeism, sabotage, and so forth.

To be effective, survey feedback efforts should be part of an ongoing program of organization development and improvement. Too many surveys are given after the fact—that is, after a problem has emerged in an organization. Surveys that take more of a diagnostic approach to organizational concerns and issues, by contrast, can provide managers with a firmer basis for confronting these issues. However, an organization that is not prepared to take action on the results is perhaps wiser *not* to undertake an attitude survey. "What, another attitude survey?" is usually the reply when employees feel that nothing has really changed since the last data-gathering exercise. Yet, by involving employees in the formulation of the program (sensing and polling sessions and interviews) and using the results (follow-up groups), an organization can become more oriented toward its future as well as significantly confront its day-to-day operational concerns.

Unfortunately, too much attitude survey work in business falls short of its potential because of cursory diagnosis, poorly constructed questionnaires, misinterpretation of the data, and/or a failure to apply this information in organization improvement efforts. The survey feedback model proposed in this book has attempted to outline for managers the process by which effective surveys can be conducted. In turn, this effort can provide an organization with a fuller indication of its strengths and weaknesses. A survey-based quality of work life assessment is not a panacea to all organizational problems. But properly used, it can increase the probability of managerial and employee involvement and effectiveness in the work place.

Endnotes

1. E.F. Huse, *Organization Development and Change* (Minneapolis: West, 1980), p. 508.
2. M.S. Cooper, B.S. Morgan, P.M. Foley, and L.B. Kaplan, "Changing Employee Values: Deepening Discontent?" *Harvard Business Review* 57:1 (1979), pp. 117–25.
3. R. Janson, "Work Redesign: A Result-Oriented Strategy That Works," in J.H. Donnelly, J.L. Gibson, and J.M. Ivancevich (eds.), *Fundamentals of Management* (Plano, Tex.: Business Publications, Inc., 1981), pp. 199–204.
4. E.F. Huse, *op. cit.*
5. E.F. Huse, and M. Beer, "Eclectic Approach to Organization Development," *Harvard Business Review* 49:5 (1971), pp. 103–12.
6. A good example of this process can be found in E.A. Mollander, *Responsive Capitalism: Case Studies in Corporate Social Conduct* (New York: McGraw-Hill, 1980); see Case 12, "Employee Participation in Improving the Quality of Work Life at General Motors," pp. 144–51.
7. C. Perrow, *Organizational Analysis: A Sociological View* (Belmont, Calif.: Brooks-Cole, 1970); H. Aldrich, *Organizations and Environments* (Englewood Cliffs, N.J.: Prentice-Hall, 1979).
8. J.D. Thompson, *Organizations in Action* (New York: McGraw-Hill, 1967).
9. D. Sirota, "Why Managers Don't Use Attitude Survey Results," in S.W. Gellerman, *Behavioral Science in Management* (Baltimore: Penguin Books, 1974), pp. 86–98.

Appendix

STATISTICAL TECHNIQUES

In the process of conducting quality of work life surveys, there will often be times when it is useful to provide a more complete quantitative analysis of the survey data than simple frequency distributions or cross-tabulations. These more sophisticated analyses are desirable when researchers wish to determine (1) which variables are related to each other, (2) whether there are differences between sub-samples of the survey that could be attributed to chance, and/or (3) whether certain attitudes are predictable by knowing the levels of other attitudes. Additionally, techniques are available to reduce the number of questions on a survey instrument yet still retain the scope or breadth of coverage within the questionnaire.

Since data are often gathered from a sample of the population of interest, most of these techniques are used to estimate which findings are applicable to the population as a whole. At times when the entire population is surveyed, some of these quantitative techniques may also be used to explore relationships between variables. The purpose of this appendix, however, is not to discuss fully each of these statistical techniques and their application. Rather, it provides an introduction to various statistical techniques that are commonly used in the analysis of quality of work life survey data and to the basic assumptions underlying these techniques.

Interval Data-Based Inferential Statistics

Because some statistical methods are quite powerful and commonly understood, most published attitude surveys based on a sample use one or more of the following techniques as part of the quantitative analysis: (1) correlations, (2) regression, (3) analysis of variance, (4) *t*-tests, and (5) factor analysis. While other statistical techniques are often employed as well, a basic understanding of these five methods will provide the researcher with sufficient background to compare their results with other studies.

All of the techniques described in this appendix are based on the following assumptions:

1. The data are interval (see pp. 114–115).

2. The data are normally distributed. Since the concept of a normal curve is fundamental to inferential statistics, the form of a frequency distribution is an important consideration in data analysis. Basically, data distributions are classified as either *symmetrical* (one half of the distribution is a mirror image of the other half) or *skewed* (if a greater accumulation of scores falls to either the right or left hand of the distribution). Figure A–1 shows (a) a normal distribution (bell shaped curve), (b) a negatively skewed distribution (a positively skewed distribution would be slanted to the left hand side of the graph), (c) a rectangular distribution, and (d) a multi-modal distribution. Although (a), (c), and (d) are all symmetrical distributions, the techniques discussed in this appendix assume a distribution along the lines of *illustration (a)*. If researchers have non-normally distributed, interval data, they can either use ordinal statistics, or use interval statistics with the expectation that the data may actually be more significant than the statistical analysis shows.

3. In addition, techniques based on *correlation* further assume a linear relationship between two variables and equal variance

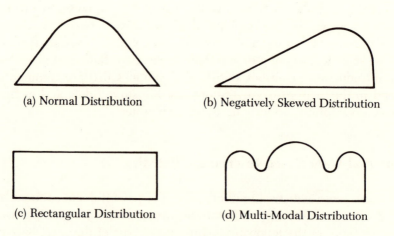

    (a) Normal Distribution   (b) Negatively Skewed Distribution

    (c) Rectangular Distribution   (d) Multi-Modal Distribution

Figure A-1   Various Frequency Distributions.

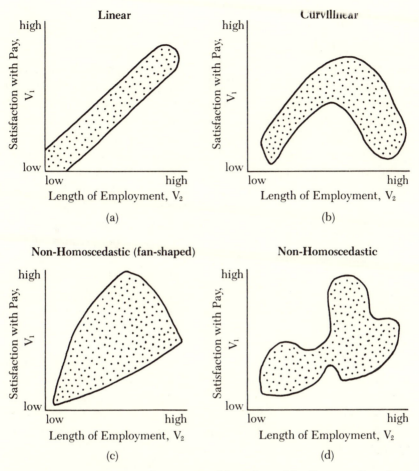

Figure A-2 Scatter Plots Showing Possible Relationships Between Length of Employment and Pay.

throughout the distribution of the two variables. Equal variance or dispersal throughout a distribution is called homoscedasticity. Figure A–2 presents different distributions of hypothesized relationships between length of employment and satisfaction with pay: (a) illustrates a linear relationship, (b) shows a non-linear or curvilinear relationship, (c) a non-homoscedastic (fan shaped) relationship, and (d) a non-homoscedastic relationship. This type of scatter plotting is useful to graphically display the relationship between two variables and, perhaps more importantly, to indicate whether the relationship is linear or non-linear.

Correlation

The first technique, which can be used either inferentially or descriptively, is referred to as correlation. Originally spelled correlation, it describes statistically the association of one interval level variable with another. As an example, we can look at a hypothetical relationship between length of time employed in an organization and satisfaction with pay. A Pearson correlation coefficient (r) would tell how much correspondence there was between the two variables, length of employment and pay. The range of possible scores is between $r = \pm 1.00$. A perfect correspondence would yield a score of $r = +1.00$, a high correlation in the range of $r = +.60$, no correlation a score $r = .00$, and a high negative correlation in the range of $r = -.60$. Figure A–3 presents some hypothetical results of the scatter plots and related correlations between length of employment and pay. For each diagram, the different dots represent each person's length of employment and satisfaction with pay. Assume, for example, that the correlation between the two variables is high. As Figure A–3 (a) shows, given a particular length of time employed, one is able to predict a narrow range of satisfaction with pay. In other words, in this instance workers who have been around a long time are more satisfied with their pay than those individuals who have been with the organization for shorter periods of employment. This type of bivariate correlation analysis provides a single summary statistic describing the relationship between the two variables. The *number* or *value* indicates the strength of the relationship, and the *sign* (+ or −) tells whether both variables ascend simultaneously, or whether one ascends when the other descends. For instance, low satisfaction with pay related to long term employment would yield a negative correlation—the *magnitude* or size (−.40, −.55, −.63, −.88, etc.) indicates the strength of the inverse relationship between the two variables.

Significance of Correlations. As part of the interpretation of correlations, statistical significance should be determined; that is, could the relationship between the two variables be due to chance. In general, significance is set at the .01 or .05 levels. This means that there is only a 1 percent or 5 percent probability, respectively, that the correlation occurred by chance.

Statistical significance depends on two factors: the *strength of the relationship* (the higher the correlation, the greater the probability

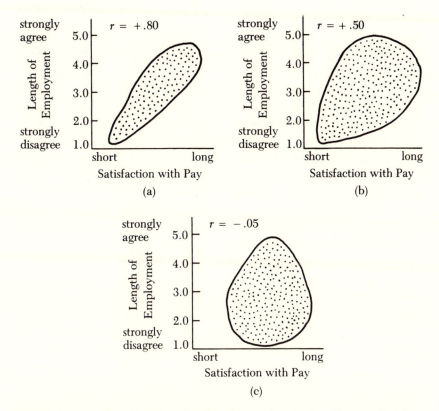

Figure A-3 Scatter Plots Showing Hypothetical Correlations Between Satisfaction with Pay and Length of Employment.

that it will be significant) and the *number of paired observations* which make up the correlation (the higher the number of pairs, the lower the required strength of the correlation in order to be significant). Statistical significance, however, should not be confused with substantive significance. If a correlation were based on a sample of 200, for instance, a value of .16 would be significant at the .05 level, not a very strong relationship.

As a *rough* guide to the value of correlations, the following system has been suggested:[1]

± .80 to 1.00	Very high correlation
.60 to .79	High correlation
.40 to .59	Moderate correlation
.20 to .39	Slight correlation
.01 to .19	Very slight correlation

Causality.   One danger in using simple correlation is to attribute causality to a relationship. For instance, if educational level and satisfaction with pay were correlated at $r = \pm.60$, one might be tempted to argue that extensive educational experience leads to or "causes" a high satisfaction in pay. Causality, however, cannot be determined by simple correlations. All that the above example indicates is that a *relationship* exists between higher levels of education and satisfaction with pay, *not* that education leads to greater pay satisfaction.* While it is possible that one leads to or causes the other, it is also possible that both variables are affected by some other variable or variables and that they do not affect each other directly.

In summary, correlational analysis is a useful tool to gain a greater understanding of the relationships between variables. It may be used between two survey questions (such as to determine the relationship of satisfaction with pay and satisfaction with benefits) or it may be used to look at the relationship between a sociodemographic index such as educational level or occupational level and satisfaction with pay. In all cases, both variables must be interval data.

Regression

Closely linked to the concept of correlation is regression analysis. Regression is used when researchers want to predict outcomes on certain variables by using another set of variables. In its simplest form, only two variables are involved, such as length of employment and satisfaction with the job. Simple regression would try to predict job satisfaction through length of time on the job. Since job satisfaction is thought to be influenced by a number of other factors, however, such a two-variable equation is unlikely to produce significant findings. Rather, we would want to look at the effect of a number of different variables such as length of employment, level of responsibility, job duties, satisfaction with pay, supervisory relationships, and so forth on job satisfaction. This process is referred to as *multiple regression*. While it is expected that multiple regression analysis should improve the predictive efficiency over simple regression,

---

* Tentative causality may be inferred from a more complex statistical procedure referred to as cross-lagged correlation, which requires a longitudinal or time-lagged framework. Since this technique is beyond the scope of the present book, the reader is encouraged to consult a statistics text.

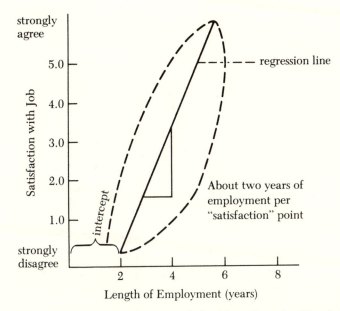

Figure A-4   Regression of Satisfaction with the Job on Length of Employment.

caution must be exercised when adding "predictor" variables. Much like the concept of "diminishing returns," there is a point where adding variables to a regression analysis will not improve its predictive effectiveness.

Three basic concepts are important for an understanding of regression analysis: the regression line, intercept, and slope. The *regression line* is the hypothetical line which goes through the center of a distribution, sometimes called the "line of best fit." If one were to add up all of the scores on a scatter plot in terms of how far above and below they fell from the regression line (scores above the line having a + value and those below having a − value), the sum would equal zero (see Figure A–4).

While the regression line goes through the middle of the distribution, the *intercept* (which is usually designated by the letter *a* or *c* in a regression equation) indicates the constant score required to make the mean (average) of one variable equal the mean of the other variable (for example, length of employment and job satisfaction). The *slope* of the distribution is the number of units of one variable needed to increase another variable by one unit. In our example, this would be the number of years of employment it takes to increase job satisfaction by one point. As indicated in Figure A–4, since the

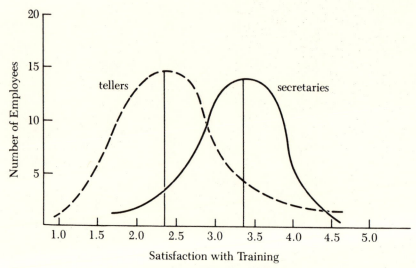

Figure A-5 Hypothetical Means and Variances of Tellers and Secretaries on Satisfaction with Training Scores.

regression line is not at a 45-degree angle, the increase in length of employment by two years increases the likelihood of job satisfaction by one point. If, on the other hand, one wished to predict in reverse, from satisfaction with the job to an estimate of how long a particular worker was employed, the regression equation would be different, with a different slope and intercept.

Regression becomes an inferential statistic when a procedure referred to as *analysis of variance* is computed for the overall regression equation. The weight associated with variables in a multiple regression, *b* (beta), provides an indication of the relative importance of the variable in the predictive efficiency of the overall regression equation. In simplified manner, such as in the assessment of job satisfaction between tellers and clerks, analysis of variance allows the researcher to compute the variance around the means of these variables. This analysis provides information as to whether tellers and clerks differ significantly with regard to expressed level of job satisfaction.

The importance of means and variance within and between distributions is reflected in Figures A–5 and A–6. Suppose we wanted to assess how tellers and secretaries within a given banking organization perceived their respective training programs. Looking at Figure A–5, it appears that tellers report a mean satisfaction level of 2.5, while secretaries report a satisfaction level of 3.0 with their training

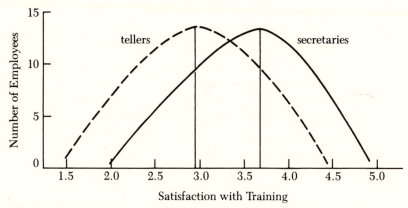

Figure A-6 Hypothetical Non-Significant Difference Between Tellers and Secretaries.

programs. It is also clear from the distribution, on the other hand, that there is an overlap between the two job clusters. Still, if a statistical test were performed on the two groups, with approximately 250 persons in each sample, a significant difference (that is, not due to chance) would be observed. However, consider the situation illustrated by Figure A–6, where the internal variance within the teller sample and the secretarial sample is much larger. In this instance, although the difference between the means is similar to that in Figure A–5, the large variance within each distribution causes so much overlap between the two groups that one could not say that tellers are significantly lower than secretaries in their average scores on the satisfaction with training question.

In summary, regression analysis indicates the relative importance of one or more variable(s) in predicting a score on some outcome variable such as job satisfaction or satisfaction with pay. Analysis of variance on regression indicates which of the predictor variables makes a significant contribution in forecasting a person's score on an outcome or dependent variable. Analysis of variance such as correlation analysis, when used as an inferential statistic, provides information as to whether the variables' contribution could be expected by chance, or whether they are significant at the .01 or .05 levels of probability.

t-Tests and F-Tests

A corollary to analysis of variance is the *t-test*. Although there is a close relationship between the two procedures, the *t*-test is used only for two-sample situations and does not apply to regression analysis. In some instances, quality of work life researchers may simply want to evaluate differences between effects, rather than the effects themselves. For example, an employer might be interested in differences in job satisfaction for people at different levels of education. One of the most common techniques for this type of analysis is a comparison of two groups, say those with a college education and those without, by using the group means as the basis for comparison. The *t*-test would indicate whether or not the difference between the two groups is statistically significant.

In multiple regression analyses and multiple correlation, F scores are used to indicate statistical significance. Since there are three possible F scores—one for the beta weight or slope, one for a subset of slopes, and one for the overall regression equation—the researcher must know whether one variable, a group of variables, or all of the independent variables involved make a significant contribution to the prediction of the outcome or dependent variable.

An *F-test (analysis of variance)* on the overall regression equation simply tests whether the population from which the sample is drawn is likely to have a multiple correlation (R) of zero (0), or whether there is a significant relationship between the predictor (independent) variables and the predicted (dependent) variables. Using the example of satisfaction with pay, satisfaction with benefits, and length of employment, if the multiple R is significantly different from 0, there will be a significant F reported.

Using Venn diagrams, possible multiple correlations between these variables are shown in Figure A–7. The schematic inference shows that the greater the overlap between the variables, the higher the multiple correlation. In fact, the square of the multiple correlation (R^2) is the amount of variance in the dependent measure accounted for by the independent measure.

Beyond a simple test of the overall regression equation, a researcher may wish to know whether some particular regression slopes (betas) add significantly to the overall regression equation. By examining the individual betas and the F scores associated with them, one can determine whether a particular variable makes a significant contribution to the overall multiple correlation.

Interactions.   When conducting an analysis of variance on an experimental design testing the manipulation of two or more variables, the researcher may find that the main manipulations of the variables do not produce any significant effect on the outcome vari-

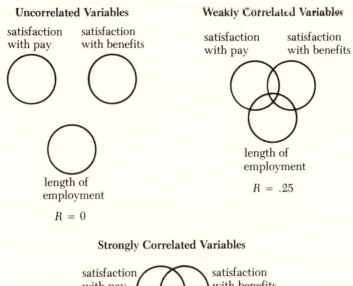

Uncorrelated Variables

satisfaction with pay   satisfaction with benefits

length of employment

$R = 0$

Weakly Correlated Variables

satisfaction with pay   satisfaction with benefits

length of employment

$R = .25$

Strongly Correlated Variables

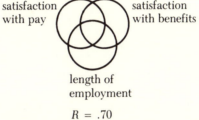

satisfaction with pay   satisfaction with benefits

length of employment

$R = .70$

Figure A-7 Venn Diagrams Showing Relationships Between Uncorrelated, Weakly Correlated, and Strongly Correlated Variables.

able, but that the combination of two or more variables does produce an effect. For example, a researcher may want to study the relationship between managerial and clerical employee job satisfaction, and the number of claim errors per week in an insurance company. Based on attitude surveys taken for all employees, two groups among the managerial and clerical categories can be formulated—those satisfied with their jobs and those who report that they are not satisfied. As indicated in Table A–1, the mean levels of errors for each group can then be compared. Based on these data, the example indicates that managerial job satisfaction appears to be a significant factor in the level of claim errors.

If, on the other hand, there was no difference in marginal totals but individual cells were obviously different, an interaction would be present. Consider the data in Table A–2. The marginal totals (15 each) represent equal numbers of mistakes under both levels of

Table A–1   Mean Number of Claim Errors in Two-by-Two Table When Worker Satisfaction Is Dominant

	Managers		
Clerical Workers	*Satisfied*	*Unsatisfied*	*Total*
Satisfied	10	10	20
Unsatisfied	5	5	10
Total	15	15	30

Table A–2   Mean Number of Claim Errors in Two-by-Two Table Where an Interaction Effect Exists Between Workers' and Managers' Levels of Job Satisfaction

	Managers		
Clerical Workers	*Satisfied*	*Unsatisfied*	*Total*
Satisfied	5	10	15
Unsatisfied	10	5	15
Total	15	15	30

satisfaction for managers and clerical workers. However, when looking at the cells, clearly something is different. This suggests that matching workers and managers with similar levels of satisfaction seems to be more effective (fewer claim errors) than having managers with different degrees of satisfaction from workers. There can be said to be a manager/worker interaction on the basis of satisfaction. In statistical tables in journal articles, such interaction will be presented as shown in Table A–3. If either the *A* or *B* main effects had been significant, an asterisk would have been placed next to the *F* in the *A* and/or *B* row.

In brief, three statistical techniques have been presented, correlation, regression, and analysis of variance. Since analysis of variance is used to test the significance of regression, it is difficult to separate the two techniques completely. An analysis of variance design without regression is customarily used in laboratory experiments and field experiments when the variables are under the control of the researchers. All of the techniques are meaningful when used in samples of populations being surveyed. When whole populations are surveyed, correlation may have some use, but analysis of variance and analysis of regression have little interpretive value because their use is predicated on the assumption that the researcher is going to generalize from a sample to a population.

Table A–3 Summary of an Analysis of Variance Table

Variable	Analysis of Variance			
	SS	df	MS	F
A (manager satisfaction)	3	1	3	1.33
B (worker satisfaction)	3	1	3	1.33
AB (interaction)	30	1	30	15*
Within group variance	398	199	2	

* p < .01

Data Reduction—Factor Analysis

Sometimes it is desirable to reduce a large number of questions on an attitude survey to a few. Once the initial set of questions has been formulated and pilot tested, it is possible to give the questionnaire to a large representative sample of persons and then perform a factor analysis to search for underlying patterns of relationship between the variables involved. When such relationships exist, the data may be reduced to a smaller set of factors or variables for analytic purposes.

Two main criteria must be accommodated for factor analysis. As discussed earlier, the data must be interval and reasonably normally distributed like a bell-shaped curve since correlations will be computed for *each* pair of attitude survey questions. Although the computation appears to be a mammoth undertaking, with computers the whole process is reasonably straightforward.

The second requirement is that there be approximately four times as many respondents as the number of questions employed. This ratio ensures that when the final factors are statistically determined, the solution is more likely to be optimal and not subject to change. Moreover, the results of a factor analysis are partially determined by the number of questions included on a given subject. Thus, if 50 percent of the items on an attitude survey asked questions about feelings toward pay, one would expect a factor or set of factors on pay to emerge.

When data are factor analyzed, a set of hypothetical dimensions are created with which the original questions are correlated. These correlations, termed "loadings," indicate how much the factor resembles any one question or group of questions. In one kind of factor analysis, the principal components method with the varimax rotation, each factor is completely independent, or *orthogonal*, from each prior factor. Each factor accounts for a percentage of variance in the overall questionnaire, and the factor which accounts for most of the variance, that is, is most influential, emerges first. The second factor accounts for the second largest amount of variance, and so forth. If one wanted to account for all of the variance in a questionnaire, one might need a number of factors equal to the number of questions on the questionnaire. However, the first few factors usually account for the bulk of the variance.

For example, Tables A–4 to A–6 present factor analysis data from an attitude survey conducted in a bank.[2] Overall, fifty-one items were included in the factor analysis based on 230 respondents. Based on this analysis, three factors emerged, accounting for 68.9 percent of the variance in employee attitudes: supervisor support, promotion and advancement opportunity, and ratings of the bank's merit and compensation systems.

As is evident from Table A–4, the first factor to emerge concerned employee relationships with supervisors. A decision was made in the research to show only those items with a loading stronger than ±35. Even though these were only a portion of the questions which dealt with supervisory relations, the importance of supervision is apparent in that almost 49 percent of the variance in employee attitudes was accounted for by this factor.

The second factor that emerged from the data concerned promotion and job satisfaction (Table A–5). Although the factor loadings include a wider collection of items, the factor is still clear in terms of the relation of items. The second factor, however, is less important than the first as it accounts for only 11.3 percent of the variance in employee attitudes.

The final factor in this analysis concerns salary determination (Table A–6). Note that in each of the factors discussed, there are fewer high loadings. This is related to the amount of variance accounted for in the data set. In the case of factor three, only four items load on the factor above .35, but their relationship is clear. It is interesting to note that although there were as many questions on pay as on supervision, the pay items did not cluster as neatly on one factor. In fact, they were spread out over four factors, the last three minor ones which accounted for very little variance. Since the top three factors account for 69 percent of the variance and, because of the loadings, it is clear what each of the factors means, it would be possible to create questions which would align themselves with one of the factors. An arbitrary decision could be made, for example, to create three questions per factor and reduce the size of the survey considerably.

Table A–4   Factor 1

Factor Title: This factor has been designated as the Supervisor-related factor. It accounted for 48.8% of the variance in employee attitudes.

Variable (abbreviated question)	Loading
My supervisor supports me.	.78952
I can talk to my immediate supervisor.	.73818
My immediate supervisor listens to me.	.70868
My supervisor understands the problems of my job.	.70484
My supervisor continues to train me.	.69738
My supervisor makes me aware of what is expected.	.68648
My supervisor sees we are trained for jobs.	.66735
I usually know how I stand.	.54105
My supervisor makes me aware of promotion opportunities.	.50854

Table A–5   Factor 2

Factor Title: This factor has been designated as the Opportunity for Promotion and Advancement related factor. It accounted for 11.3% of the variance in employee attitudes.

Variable (abbreviated question)	Loading
Opportunity here for anyone to get ahead.	.68647
Promotions given to those who deserve.	.64630
Promotion policy from within works well.	.63430
Positive action will come from survey.	.56431
Sense of pride in working for the bank.	.52130
Overall I am satisfied with my job.	.51814
Best suited for job I am doing.	.50218
Opportunity for career advancement provided.	.49612
My work is worthwhile and important.	.48555
I can say what I think without fear.	.39960
No discrimination in advancement.	.35756
Job safe as long as done satisfactorily.	.35098

Table A–6   Factor 3

Factor Title: This factor was designated as the Understanding of Merit System and Compensation Plan related factor. It accounted for 8.8% of the variance in employee attitudes.

Variable (abbreviated question)	Loading
Understand salary classification system.	.74339
Have been informed of job salary range.	.70070
Understand merit system workings.	.64756
Periodic rating system is good.	.40917

Summary

This appendix has illustrated the use of the major statistical techniques which treat interval data. All of the procedures are available through a number of statistical packages already programmed for the computer. One which we find particularly useful is N. H. Nie, et al., *Statistical Package for the Social Sciences*. In addition to containing most available statistical analysis techniques appropriate for interval data, as well as techniques for the analysis of other levels of data, both the descriptions of the techniques and the formats of data presentation are very clear.

Endnotes

1. B. Turney and G. Robb, *Research in Education: An Introduction* (Hinsdale, Ill.: Dryden Press, 1971), pp. 99–100.
2. J.J. O'Neil, "A Factor Analytic Study of Employee Attitudes at a Medium-Sized Savings Bank," unpublished bachelor's thesis, Boston College, School of Management, 1978.

SUBJECT INDEX

Action research, 42–46
Alpha change, 129
Analysis of variance, 159–60, 161t
Anticipative management, 49–51, 144–46
Attitude surveys (*see also* Qualitative data analysis; Quantitative data analysis)
  administration of, 103–106
  and anonymity, 31, 56, 60–61, 87
  data analysis, 107–37, 149–64
  data coding, 110–12
  data editing, 108–10
  data gathering devices, 30–39
  data interpretation, 125–27
  descriptive data, 127–28
  development of questionnaire, 64–80 (*see also* Questionnaire development)
  and external environments, 143–46
  feedback, of survey results, 131–34
  implementation of survey procedures, 83–106
  and industry norms, 58–59, 130–31
  instructions, 96, 97–102f, 103
  introductory letter, 85–88, 90–92f
  linkage of qualitative and quantitative data analyses, 124–25
  ongoing feedback efforts, 136–37
  organizational follow-up, 134–36
  pilot testing, 55–56, 79–80
  results over time, 128–30
  and threat of unionization, 61
  timetable for, 83–85, 86t
  training survey administrators, 104–105
  utilization of results, 134–36
Attitude survey planning, 55–64, 112–113
  organizational climate, 62
  preliminary diagnosis, 61–64
  sensing groups, 62–64
Attitude survey question wording, 75–78
  double barreled questions, 77
  leading questions, 77
  misleading questions, 77–78
  response sets, 75–77
Attitude survey response forms, 88–89, 93f, 94, 95f
  direct response, 88–89, 94, 95f, 96, 100–102f
  optical scanning, 88–89, 94, 96, 97–99f
Attribution theory, 17
  and survey interpretation, 126
Attributional biases, 17

Beta change, 129
Boundaries, organizational, 4–5

Closed-ended questions, 71–73, 94–95
  coding of, 110–11
Closed systems, 5
Coercive power base, 9–10
Collages and drawings, as data gathering devices, 32–33t, 39
Commitment and organizational power structures, 9–10
Consultants, external vs. internal, 56–59, 60t
Content analysis, 111
Cornell Job Description Index, 34
Correlation, 149–54
Cross-tabulation of survey data, 116–18
Cyclical Planned Intervention Model, 20, 39–51, 47f

AUTHOR INDEX

Note: The page number(s) given for each entry refers to the page in the text where the author's name is mentioned or his work discussed. Superior reference numbers are keyed to the endnotes following each chapter. The reader may consult the endnotes for full bibliographic information.